Sketches

INCLUDING

Ingrid's Story

E. K. WILLIAMS

Published by
CATTAIL PRESS
150 Baltusrol Road
Fairfield Glade, TN 38558

First Edition 2011

ISBN: 978-0-578-08009-3
Library of Congress Control Number: 2011903650

ABOUT THE BOOK

What are sketches? There are sketches made with pencils or paint, those that depict architectural layouts, even those short little musical tunes that are sometimes referred to as compositions; but my sketches are composed entirely of words. The entire sketch may be long or short (usually on the short side), heavy with pathos (generally, not so with mine) or light with wit and silliness (more so like mine).

A sketch may present one or both sides of an argument or view point, thereby appearing similar to the essay format. It may sound like a short story, but may sometimes lack the climax of the events and even found to be missing the denouement so it may just slide and unfold into a plausible resolution. And gadzooks, please spare us the verse that trips over its own rhyme, and may accidentally even be mistaken for a poem, though generally, all it may provoke is a laugh, a groan, a giggle or a moan. One never knows for sure. One thing is true, the arrangement of my "Sketches" in this book is all mixed up according to the style of the piece: one page may sound like a poem while the very next page may be just plain old story telling. My "Sketches" are grouped according to the content of each sketch. For instance, those works that are primarily about nature are grouped under "Taking a Stroll," and those dealing with opposing view points are listed under "On Second Thought….." and so on. You'll catch on.

Sketches are not demanding or strict in style and for those who are adamant perfectionists with regard to rules and such, may experience a bit of annoyance. But once past such little stumblings (indeed, if any at all) just lean back, take a deep breath or two and enjoy journeys into reality, fantasy and dreams.

I'm not at all sure how Ingrid got into this book at this time and at this place. Ingrid has been around for awhile. I would be finishing a sketch on a certain subject, going along nicely, thank you, and along comes Ingrid.

"Now, wait just a minute, Ingrid," I would scold. "I would really be grateful if you didn't pop into my mind right now, just as I'm finishing this piece about a rooster. How will I ever get it done?"

"Oh, I know," Ingrid would respond, "but if I don't remind you about my exciting and unusual stories, you might forget them, and….."

"Ok, you're right. I'll just write about the scary dollhouse and I can finish the rooster later."…..and, so it would go, leaving me to wonder: how will I assemble these different and unique pieces, or sketches, so they would make sense? I discovered the answer I needed. I would allow stories about Ingrid to visit as they pleased, make a note about them, set them aside and when time allowed, I would put them all together, as you would with pieces of a puzzle, and hopefully they would spell out the sequential tales of a young girl's life.

It worked. The sketches of various subjects stood by themselves and Ingrid's stories just seemed to flow, one into the other. In fact, even now as we chat, there are more tales about Ingrid, waiting in the wings, waiting to be heard, taking their place in line…….

DEDICATIONS

This book is dedicated with loving gratitude to my husband, Joe, for his understanding, affection and constancy while supporting my endeavors.

To our son, Christian, our daughter-in-law, Debby, and granddaughters Aryn and Erica I dedicate this, my second book, along with a special sense of appreciation for their loving enthusiasm for my writings.

Further dedications are extended to my stepdaughter, Lori, and her husband, Jack; to my stepdaughter, Liz, her husband, Mike, and our granddaughter, Calleigh, who have all expressed their joy with my book. I also dedicate this book to my stepson, Charles, and grandson, Colin.

This book, especially, "Ingrid's Story" is dedicated to my family of origin, my parents, Boris and Gudren Jespersen, who left their homeland in Denmark, and raised a family in the traditions of both their birthplace and America. My book is also dedicated to my oldest sister, Bea, her husband, Helge, who is now deceased and their four children, Linda, Cheryl, Karen and Mark, and their families.

My book, *Sketches* is further dedicated to my sister, June, now deceased, and her husband, Fred, and their three children, Lisa, Amy and Jessica and their families. A heartfelt dedication is extended to my two brothers-in-law, Doug and Gordon and to my two sisters-in-law, Marg and Fran, for their support and encouraging comments about my new book.

I am especially grateful that I have been able to put some words together in the hopes that they may be meaningful as well as enjoyable to you, the reader; and I thank you for allowing me, even for a brief moment, to enter your life.

ACKNOWLEDGEMENTS

I wish I could acknowledge all of the kind folks who influenced and inspired the writing of my second book, *Sketches*. However, here's a brief list that includes a never-ending expression of gratitude: to Alan Philips, Ph.D.for his inspiration and unconditional positive regard; to dear friends: Irene Wiren, Bonnie Richter and Lou Teal. Special gratitude is due to Wendy Reed, Don Beck and Jim Byars for their ongoing special encouragement. A note of thanks is extended to Krista Kemmer for her work and to Jane Komar for her achievements. Linda Petersen, my niece and my son, Christian, have always been available for invaluable input and comments. Further thanks are extended to Dean Hutson, publisher of "Our Senior Times" for including my works in every month's edition and to Michael Northen, Editor of Wordgathering, for selecting my works for his journal. I also extend my gratitude to editor/ author, Carla Richards and author/editor, Ina Hughs for their kind evaluation of my first book.

It is due, in part to the positive pat on the back, "Job well done" encouragement that I received that brought *Sketches* to its conclusion as well as a prompting for a new beginning.

CONTENTS

To Be Brief...

Ingrid's Story

Out to Dinner

"Good evening, Mr. & Mrs. Jones. Welcome to Park Place restaurant. We have your reserved table waiting for you. This way please."

"Thank you. My, you sure are crowded tonight."
"Yes, yes, we are. Ah, here's your table. Hope this is satisfactory. Enjoy your dinner."

(*From a table to the right*):*"Abortion? I know my cell phone may not be working right, but, come on, did you really say that? She can't do that! I don't care if it is legal morally, it's just not right. Her friends won't stand for it and come to think of it – neither will I – and I'm going to tell her so too."*

"Good evening, my name is Jane and I'll be your server this evening. Can I get you something from the bar?"

(from a table to their left): "Hey hi honey, boy I thought I'd get out of the office before now, but looks like I'm stuck here and going to be late. You go ahead with dinner and don't wait up for me. What, of course, I'm calling you from the office…… I'm using the cell 'cause it's handy."

"I'll have a chardonnay and the lady will have a merlot."
"Yes sir. I'll get those for you right away. By the way, the special tonight is . . ."

(*table behind theirs*): *"So, like now, I grab my cell phone and I tell him:* ***YOU CAN TAKE THIS JOB AND SEND IT YOU KNOW WHERE, THAT'S WHAT I TOLD HIM….***

I mean, I've been with this company and made you lots of.."

"Tripe, yes sir, tripe or salmon. I'll go over the rest of the menu with you in a moment, after I order your drinks." "Isabelle, you sure look lovely tonight," John remarked. That dress really does something for....you....

(from a nearby table): "I think they should go ahead with the divorce, I'm not sorry I did. I wish they'd bring my dessert soon. Listen, I'm getting tired of talking to a cell phone. I'm going to have to hang or this one's going to die out on me……."

"Ah, here come our drinks. What do you say to a steak, or maybe something in a good fish, like –

(3 tables over): …:Mother, I just can't talk right now. I'm on my cell in a busy restaurant. I'm sure the pink dress will be ok, .whoops, I've got another call coming in – will get back to you later."

"Here are your drinks. Would you folks like to order now?

(From a table somewhere): " I'll have to call back with the details, I just finished my liver loaf and pureed squash and they just served my dessert. It's berry shortcake, chocolate ice cream, fudge sauce, caramel syrup…"

Jane, I'm not sure, for some reason or another, my appetite seems to be dwindling. Have you decided what you would like tonight, dear?"
"I'll just have the chicken special and a salad."
"Why don't you just double that?"
"Certainly, sir. That'll be right up."

(*Table directly in front*): ***"THREW UP . . . THAT'S WHAT HAPPENED! THE WHOLE FAMILY.*** *They went to eat in that new place in town and the food must have been rancid or rotten and they threw up for days. Had the runs, too, all of them. Can you imagine? Oh, here's Mike and Alice, yoo hoo, over here, I'd better hang up my cell...... I'll call you tomorrow."*

"Sorry for the wait, sir. Here are your dinners."
"Jane, before we start to enjoy our wonderful dinners, I would like you to go to the kitchen and bring me a large, clean, roasting pan, and if there's a problem with that, just ask the manager to drop by and see me."
"Here's the pan, sir. The manager said he was sure that a long standing, good customer like you must have a good reason to see our roasting pan."
"Thank you, Jane"
"John, what are you doing?"
"Isabelle, I'm putting this large spoon into my coat pocket so it will look like a gun. It is not a gun or a weapon of any sort and I am completely harmless, but now, bear with me, I'm going to stand up and shout:

" OK FOLKS – I NEED YOUR ATTENTION HERE...I'M GOING TO STOP BY EACH OF YOUR TABLES AND YOU WILL DEPOSIT YOUR CELL PHONE INTO THIS PAN. I HAVE A GUN IN MY POCKET THAT SAYS YOU WILL DO THIS – NOW! Thank you. Thank you....YOU MAY PICK UP YOUR PHONE FROM YOUR SERVER BEFORE YOU LEAVE. THANK YOU. THANK YOU FOR YOUR COOPERATION. MY WIFE AND I ARE NOW

GOING TO SIT DOWN AND ENJOY OUR DINNER. THANK YOU FOR NOT SHARING YOUR PERSONAL LIVES WITH US UNTIL WE ARE FINISHED. THANK YOU.

(BY: CUSTOMER DAYDREAMING
WHILE WAITING FOR DESSERT.)

A New Year's Resolution – Maybe

Holidays make it hard to resist the bulging buffets
That are tempting all of us to go astray
From whatever diet you may be following right now,
For no matter how you slice it, dice it, or who knows how
You face it, there are rules by which we must abide
In order to squeeze, zip, button or set aside
The smaller clothes that fit before the holidays arrived
So we'll decide, here and now, upon which regimen we'll abide

The most arduous regimen is a bitter pill to swallow:
called EX- ER-CIZE-- -UGH! (Can't I start that tomorrow?)
It's an activity that comes in many guises,
Like fat machines and skinny ropes and bar bells in many sizes.
But if you're brave, you'll kid yourself into going to the gym
and maybe hire a trainer who says you'll get trim:
Who'll coax, cajole and demand, "One more set,"
And we pray as we try, just maybe he'll forget.

The bravest of us all are those who enter the inner doors,
To the *pool* in a swimsuit to exercise some more
But the awful truth will surface, no matter how you soak it,
There's no swimsuit on earth that can cover more than it's supposed to.

So, the holidays are upon us, and now I think I'll say with glee -
Let's have pheasant, a goose and that bird in the pear tree
And twelve days of Christmas, nay – bring on thirteen
And we'll carol as we open gifts for nine hours in-between
Feasting on plum pudding, sweets and raspberry surprise.

On Second Thought...

You bring the turkey, we'll all bake some pies.
And when the New Year cometh, we're sure to discover
that we all gained a few pounds and there's a bit more to cover -
But not to fret,'cause as we clearly agreed
We can swim and bike, and buy a new suit, size 33 (and ½.)

Don't Clap 'til It's Over

Music fulfills a number of purposes. It is written, performed and listened to for our enjoyment, relaxation and meditation. It is used for romantic settings, funeral settings, particular religious events, specific ceremonies and celebrations, some dance music, and then, remember that long list of: "Music to Dine To, Music to Dance To, Music To......(you fill in the blank) To," and so on. Where would the ballet be, or musical theater, or numerous other artistic pursuits, sans music? .

Music and I have always been buddies, best of chums, you might say. I prefer classical, but enjoy many other forms and styles. Inasmuch as I swore I would never write a "how to" article, I've noticed certain customs, practices and behaviors while attending concerts of classical music by a symphony orchestra, which might be fun to share with you, but a warning, is only fair. I've been in an irreverent mood lately and I find that principles I once took quite seriously seem to be gradually diminishing in their importance as I advance in years. Perhaps it's because, as I get to know myself, I take myself less seriously and find life to be closer to a "looney tune" than a dirge.

For openers, did you know that Mozart was tone deaf? Or was that Beethoven? No matter, Mozart was still known as a "baby prodigy," playing piano and composing at six months old. I was not. I waited until age five, when I was old. I started composing the first time I touched a piano. I played two notes: one note to begin the composition and one note to end it. That's all you ever really need, you know, a one note beginning and a one note ending. All the rest of the stuff in between is just filler.

Jumbled up, mixed up notes that just hop and stumble around and ramble here and there, not knowing if they're supposed to be loud or soft, legato or staccato, fast or slow or sharp or flat. Well, as you can see, there's no end to what the notes can do and the composers know that, but they think you, the listener, want to hear the filler, because we clap so much when the piece is over. The composer thinks we clap because we liked it, not because we're relieved it's over.

Whoops, didn't mean to end this before we even get started. The beginning of a concert goes like this. Just when all the musicians are assembled on the stage, have finished their last minute practicing (you would think they'd know the music by now) out walks this special fellow, usually in tails, stands in front of all the musicians and faces the audience, and without doing anything, everybody claps and he takes a bow! (I'll tell you one thing, if you or I did that, I don't think people would start clapping.) I've understood, however, that this fellow is the leader, or the conductor, and knows all the music which is why they clap for him. He'll stand up on the podium, and when he waves a thin stick (baton), the musicians play and when he doesn't wave it, you're right, they don't play.

I can't help but scan the audience (it's an excellent people watching place) and wonder why so many folks attend a concert? There are many reasons and to name but a few: 1) We go to the concert to please someone else. 2) We attend the concert to keep someone company. 3) We go to be seen by others, because 4) We want others to think we love classical music, and 5) We love classical music.

Since concerts are so well attended, I do have a few ideas that might encourage some changes in the concert format or procedures, offered in hopes of increasing your listening pleasure.

First: All concerts are too long, with the exception of opera. That is because all those famous composers wrote too many compositions, therefore; Second: No composer should be allowed to write more than one composition. That way, everyone could have a chance to hear his/her piece played and concerts would not be allowed to last for more than one hour. Even that one hour can be difficult. Have you ever looked around the concert hall and noticed that hardly anyone moves (or twitches) at least not more than a few degrees to the left or right? That's because it's not allowed. Moreover, if you should become emotionally elated or excited with the music as it finally reaches its tumultuous melodic climax and you feel driven to stand up and shout, "Hooray!" – don't you dare move! It simply is not allowed! Although I've spied a couple here and there who have exchanged little Mona Lisa smiles! Third: If every composer only wrote his one piece, all of us would have a much better chance of identifying it when we hear it played, such as: "Oh, I know that piece, that's the one piece written by Gerard Millingham Worthington, Opus 343, in the key of G major (including a modulation to e minor), consisting of five movements, written in July of 2003, and dedicated to his mother. Now, doesn't that make us sound absolutely tremendously well-informed, and the other benefit of the one piece limit is that we'll all get to know that piece so well that during a performance, or concert, we'll know exactly when it's over, and as a group we'll only clap at the end. You say, you don't know what I mean? If you've ever been the poor unfortunate bloke who loudly and enthusiastically clapped by himself when the piece was only half over, you would know what I mean. (The unwritten rule is: never clap between movements (or sections) of a composition, only at the end. How do you know when it's over? You wait for someone else to start clapping.) On second thought, I just had a second thought. Why not print the words "clap here" at the appropriate places on the program? I'll bet you would have a 100% appreciative audience, breathing a sigh, in unison, of relief. Fourth: Another reason for the one piece per composer is we will all get to know the music very well. Isn't it true, that we all smile a little bit whenever we hear a familiar piece, maybe even remarking, "Oh, listen to the beautiful melody, don't you just love it?" Instead, because we have such a surplus of music, we hear much more music that we don't know, have never even heard of before and when we do hear it, we actually grimace and show a frown of disapproval upon our face. Not long ago, an orchestra played a fairly contemporary selection, meaning written within the past 50 years. It had a unique melody, or combination of sounds and unfamiliar harmonies. The reception of the music was something akin to an uninvited stranger barging into a room full of invited guests. The new fellow had simply not withstood the test of time and we, in the audience could barely lightly touch our hands together (a timid sort of clap) to show our lack of appreciation. We were actually snooty, acting superior and looking down our disdainful, collective noses at this upstart, this, this – "enfant terrible."

However, is it not our personal privilege to pick and choose our musical preferences? Of course, but do most of us have to stay married to the works of Bach, (1685-1750), Beethoven (1770-1827) and Brahms (1833-1897)? I'm not suggesting a divorce, but isn't a token of our undying faithfulness, having preferred a specific style of music for a period of 212 years during which these fellows recorded their genius, sufficient homage - commencing 325 years ago? From the Baroque period to the present date of 2010, it appears we have been stuck – musically speaking, that is.

I appreciate that excellent music survives the test of time, but, I, for one, in addition to the old favorites, would like to hear compositions reflective of our present era, where the music is more fitting of our times, as the music of the Baroque age was to itself. In addition to the "three B's" listed above, how about including three more "B's:" Barber, Samuel (1910-1981), Bartok, Bela (1881-1945), and Berstein, Leonard (1918-1990). Interesting that we do not inflict such tenacity upon styles of architecture, vehicles, clothing, or art, at least not to the extent we consign to music.

However, if you are ready to take the daring plunge into new and different sounds, ask your computer or library for the names of contemporary classical composers. Get a few tapes and listen to one tape at least ten times (not in succession) without daydreaming, without solving problems or without multi-tasking and decide if you like it well enough to listen to it again. Sorry, but it does take that long for the brain and ear to become accustomed to the new sounds.

Then, the next time you attend a concert that includes selections of contemporary classical music, perhaps you'll be accustomed to the sounds and willing to open that door a little bit wider and welcome the uninvited stranger with a resounding round of applause, because you think you might possibly like that music and not because it's over. (Just remember when to clap!)

(P.S. I just received information that a designated person will be assigned to monitor the attendees during a concert and should a patron fall asleep during the performance, his seat number will be submitted to the proper concert and seating authorities.)

When Age Comes to Call

I'm not at all sure what age is. I see other folks tote those years around. They tell me it happened all of a sudden. They say they awoke one morning and there they were – those years – they were just there, and that's how it all started. One gal said she awoke with a whole bunch of it. That it was given to her and that she never even asked for it. She tried to find out where she could return them (those extra years), but if anyone knew, they weren't telling.

Sometimes age seems to be like a pest, always hanging around, not really wanted, and a real nuisance. Come to think of it, guess it's always been here, but we looked at it differently. There was a time when we couldn't wait for the arrival of more age; *oh, for just one more year! or maybe two! then we could do all those wild and exciting things!* (that never really became very wild or exciting). There were times we wanted those extra years so badly, we were even tempted to stretch the truth about our actual number of years. Then gradually, we seemed to reach a place where we actually became comfortable about our age. Where we were was ok, but as I recall, that didn't last very long.

At one point we seemed to board a train that was rather slow moving; we had good seats and excellent views of the scenery passing by. The meals on board were wonderful and the service was perfect. Then, something strange happened. The train, ever so gradually, started going faster. The scenery started to go by too quickly. And we were rushed trying to eat our dinner. Finally and without any warning, the train seemed to whiz by, way beyond the speed limit, traveling much too fast to catch the lovely views and with hardly any time for dinner. In one way, we were fortunate we could go so far so fast, but did we really have time to enjoy the ride? I hope so, because the ride has not slowed down. Indeed it has accelerated so that some days I barely catch the train, board it and suddenly have to get off again.

One older senior confessed that every time he looks around, they're there. More ages behind him, in front of him, to either side of him, perhaps waiting, it seems, for an invitation because, as he says, "I sure didn't ask them to come in."

I'm beginning to think that these happenings, these ages that just show up, whenever and wherever they please, *are* contagious and without regard to gender or origin, and I had better start thinking of what to do with them.

I understand that some of the years just zip in, look around, don't really take up residence, but are more or less deciding whether or not to return. Well, I agree with the older senior fellow; they can look around all they like, but I'm sure not extending any invitation either.

I've also heard that this aging business can really slow down, and for no reason at all, start to meander and wander about, not quite sure where to settle or what to do. Something like: "Is this an aging day, or not? Is this a day I feel ten years younger or twenty years older?"

"Well," I wondered, "if that's the case," I asked one of my older friends, "If those years are going to slow down, maybe even sit down, why not see if you can store some of them?"

Several days later my friend returned and said, "I tried stuffing some of them into a dresser drawer, then into a box in the garage and later under my bed, but they always found a way out and then found me, and you should know, they're rather resistant to being stuffed – anywhere!"

At this point, I was beginning to believe that dealing with aging can pose to be a problem. In fact, guess I should admit, that lately, I'm starting to trip over some extra years that are lying around and I asked (and this is just between you and me), if they couldn't just leave or at least let me stock pile them and then take them out when I'm ready to try them on. You know, just to see how they'll fit.. In no uncertain terms I was informed that rules are rules, no storing, no stockpiling, no returns and no refunds. (Sorry, I can't reveal my source of information.) Wouldn't you have expected a clause in the initial agreement, where you could approach the GDTA (the Great Distributor of Time and Aging) and say something like, "Excuse me, but I don't like the way I used the past eight years. Could I exchange them for something different, something, say, of lighter mood or cheerier countenance?" Receiving no response, I assumed that the answer was in the negative.

All of my questions were of no avail and I had no better understanding of aging that I ever had. When, finally, after speaking at length with numerous folks, I was able to sort through the pieces and put together what I think is an exciting equation or explanation of a connection between aging and memory. It seems that a strange turn of events happen whenever a senior adult receives additional age. It is said that inside one's head a memory bank that has been sealed off for many years, dusts itself off and resurfaces, delivering a pleasurable memory with details of an event of long ago and in Technicolor. The equation would go something like this: age ----to senior----triggers memory bank to open----pleasurable memory is released----with details and in color…senior ages a few more days, but----enjoys the pleasurable recall *and* receives what is almost like an extension to his life (!). For even though the recall gift of memory has been experienced before, isn't it still being experienced all over again, in a different time frame, a different place?

An added little perk of this equation is, that when the memory bank is "dusted off" the replay will seem like just yesterday, making the gift of recall a lovely trade for a few more days (or minutes, or months) of aging. (Maybe that's why older folks will say, "Why, it seems like just yesterday, that ……..."

Adults are made of things like aging, reality, memory and recall; but children - well, I know it doesn't make sense, but I have a hard time envisioning children aging. I know they do, but there is an essence about them that whispers of eternity, and I see them as filled with tinker bell songs and wind chime melodies played in hidden places filled with secrets and surprises, skipping on the sidewalk and tossing a red rubber ball into the sun. No, children are not included in the equation of aging and memory.

Children are fairy tales and rainbows reaching over new spring meadows. They are the vision today that becomes the memory we see in our tomorrows. Come nightfall, they are the silent sounds we hear in our dreams and imaginings...Come daylight, they are the subtle, sensitive, perceptions that begin each new dawn. And perhaps, one day, their childlike visions will merge with our adult reality.

You Did What on New Year's Eve?

You watched a big ball slide down the side of a long stick? OK, uh huh, sounds like that was really a lot of fun. Yes sir, that ball went right down that pole, did it? What I'd like to know is, was there an encore? I mean, did the ball only go down the stick once? Oh, I see, it will not do it again until next year. Well, that certainly is a long time to wait for a repeat performance, but if it's worth waiting for, then you certainly wouldn't want to miss a second look at that thrilling experience. Next time around you might want to check the absence of the element of suspense because 1) You know where the ball is going, 2) You know how long its going to take to get there and 3) You know what will happen when it arrives. Other than that, it sure is an interesting story.

It is written that the explanation for the ball and stick show dates back to 1833 when some fellows in Greenwich, England concocted the idea of a ball dropping to signify the hour of 1:00 for the purpose of providing a standard measurement of time to be used in navigation and what in blazes does all that mean? I have absolutely no idea...so I refer you to the appropriate information sources. (Moreover, the discovery of an answer requires more time than is allotted herein and somehow, I suspect it would be rather boring...so, continuing on a lighter note, sans scientific knowhow.....) Initially, the ball was equipped with light bulbs and it was much later that the ball was upgraded to lights reflecting on Waterford crystal and finally, weighing in at approximately 11,000 lbs. In those referenced earlier days, approximately 150 balls were distributed around the world, but today the practice no longer exists and that is just about the only positive thing I can see about what was once referred to as a "time - ball." In its initial days, did we have Eastern Standard Time, Central Standard Time and Time-Ball Standard time???? It seems that we have been breathing life into an ancient tradition because we don't know how else to announce the New Year. Although fireworks and music have their place, which we can look at later. An additional comment about our ritual that confuses me is don't we usually hike something *up* a flag pole, like "raise the flag, boys," and it's in times of *mourning* that we *lower* whatever is on the pole, and in this case, it's not a flag, it's a ball and when it's hits bottom, we're happy, which is contrary to the common conception of feelings when someone/something has "hit bottom." Oh, my goodness, can you imagine Times Square when the ball is about to reach its bottom, if someone were to yell out, "Here comes the "time-bomb – whoops, I mean time-*ball*" Good decision the committee had about dropping the title of the ball.

It takes one minute for the ball to descend at which time we all yell, "Happy New Year." I bet the original thinkers who put this program together (I'll call it the ball and stick idea) had a real problem of how to occupy that one minute other than sit and stare at the pole while the ball is descending, until someone with a sudden inspiration, blurted out, *"I know – count!!* Of course, when in doubt have everyone count aloud!! One poor fellow on the committee, who unfortunately wasn't paying attention, said: "Count what?" Perhaps some ideas that were discarded were: 1) someone could do a dance on top of the ball while it was finding its way to the bottom, or 2) observe a minute of silence, but that idea faded cause most of the thinkers were already tired and sleepy and had to be awakened in order to continue the brainstorming session. Now - here's the real surprise: this aforementioned committee finalized their plan and "got the ball rolling" back in 1907! I had no idea! I had no idea that this remarkable example of innovative brainstorming that provided all the excitement of a ball falling down a stick can provide, has been repeating itself for 103 years!!! Do you, or *anyone*, really mean to tell me that all of the brightest idea men (and women), brilliant IQ men (and women), out there in our world, the crème of the top, the top of the top, the crème de la crème (!) have not *topped* the ball and stick routine? I think fireworks would provide much more visual and audio excitement and more appropriate to the occasion than a "plunck" or "thud" or whatever sound an approximate 11,000 lb. ball makes when it lands, hoping it doesn't make a crash landing. I wonder what kind of sound that would make and what about how many years of bad luck the recipient would receive with that much glass - probably be for the rest of an average life-span.

Moreover, it's (the ball) not romantic. I think the practice of planting a midnight kiss upon your sweetie is just fine, but in order to get the timing just right you really need to rely upon the *sound* of the actual counting for perfect timing, and not the *sight* of the ball falling. If you have to watch the ball, you'll need to stare at it, meaning assuming the right position for the kiss, stare at the ball, get up close to your sweetie, look cross-eyed at one another so you can keep looking at the ball and do the smooch exactly at the right moment. Doesn't sound very romantic to me.

Speaking of kissing, one mistake I am sure you did not make was to actually kiss anyone, no matter how briefly or lightly, at the stroke of midnight, *who does not answer to the name of your spouse,* unless you had arranged, prior to the event, separate eating and sleeping arrangements for the remainder of the year.

How about delivery of the New Year's first (supposedly) kiss timed by the music, which traditionally is "Auld Lang Syne? The proper procedure for this method is to be near, (such as dancing with) the person you want to kiss, acting kind of cool or nonchalant and when the music starts to play "Auld Lang Syne, that's your cue. Usually, there are a good number of boisterous folk who will take care of the counting aloud for you. Amazing how many natural leaders first discovered their talent and ambition by taking over the beginning of the count for the entrance of the New Year.

This past New Year's eve, you did not, once again, sing Auld Lang Syne and sound like this:?

Shood awe aquainance be fergod
An nevr braw ta mine
Shood aw aquainance be fergod
An fer days of aw lane zine. Fer aw lane zine mydear, fer awlanezine.....*and not have any idea, whatsoever, what you were singing?*

Just what does Auld Lang Syne mean? Many, or most, of us have been singing it since we were kids and have very little idea of what we're singing. What you do is just kind of mumble the words together, sing it loudly, like everyone else, smile and look real happy. Nobody will know the difference. (By the way, it's about friends who have parted and meet again.) The song is derived, somewhat, from an old Scottish folk song and it seems that Robert Burns also had his hand in the lyrics.

Oh no, you didn't accept an invitation to dinner on New Year's Day without asking, very politely, for a hint of the dinner menu? Certain dishes, popular with certain nationalities and dishes typical of regional cuisines, may be a bill of fare that can be a bit difficult to digest, especially, if you're unaccustomed to, for instance, sauerkraut that has been home made, in buckets, then later put into tubs and stomped repeatedly by the bare-footed host and hostess, (not while you're there; they'll have it done before you arrive). It can be quite tasty and with a definite homemade flavor. Another surprise might have been a lutefisk, which some Scandinavians regard as a delicacy, once it has been soaked in a salt solution in the bathtub for a day or two and typically served with meatballs and cabbage on New Year's Day. On the other hand, it's more fun to accept the invitation and be surprised. There are always antacids.

You Did What on New Year's Eve? You say that just the two of you stayed home and:

• Prepared a lobster dinner, chilled some champagne, toasted the New Year and later engaged in remarkably good will toward one another?

• Settled in for the evening with book, music, lit fireplace, made some cocoa, toasted at midnight (Central) and curled up 'neath the comforter?

• Had eggnog, listened to music, relaxed by the tree lights, retired around ten, grateful to be here for another New Year.

(Spouse especially grateful 'cause tomorrow's weather is predicted to be unusually warm with chance of possible …… *golf…..*

OR - - - Oh No, You say that the two of you or the one of you: didn't stay at home, but went out, after all these years, and continued the same old sorry behaviors in which millions of revelers have done since the days of the Romans? So, your consumption was a bit on the excessive side, just think how busy you'll be in the morning writing all those New Year's resolutions.

When Dreams Don't Come True

I've started this piece ten times, and I'm still not sure if I should write it. I'm the one who believes in gossamer dragonfly wings and elves and gnomes sliding down silvery moonbeams as the clock in the old tower peals the bewitching hour that echoes through the fog in the dark sleepy marshes. As I'm usually a positive person, who attempts to deliver a few chortles, knee-slappers and giggles, why am I writing about dreams that don't come true? Maybe it's easier to look at and write about the lighter side – it's certainly more fun. But what about our darker side? Is it to be ignored? Not at all – and that can be the problem. Just the anticipation of facing our old unresolved issues, (dreams/nightmares, or tragic events of our lives) to search inside our deepest self, is enough to send waves of fear shivering through some people to such a degree that many of us will avoid at any cost, the inward journey that might lead us to answers we're not sure we can handle.

There are some folks, who for long periods of time, would mourn their dreams that never came true, and become stuck in-between "letting go" and accepting their losses, or continuing to stay locked in with disappointment and sadness.

"When you wish upon a star…anything your heart desires, will come to you." "If you wish for something hard enough and long enough, it will come true." "Somewhere over the rainbow…and the dreams that you dare to dream really do come true."

Wouldn't it be simple and oh, so charming, if such naiveté

were true? When we were children, we probably believed that dreams came true. If something we wished for materialized, by coincidence, then that would have qualified as a "dreams come true..." However, it was long ago when in our secret fantasies, we listened to the crickets sing at nightfall and in the morning, we tipped-toed out to the back porch and while everyone was asleep, we blew bubbles and sent them floating high on a breeze against a blue sky, catching the sun's prismatic rays. And long ago when we wanted something so bad, we said we "could taste it." In support of the dream theory, weren't we also told "If you want something hard enough and long enough, it will come to you," and if you persevere, there's nothing you can't do? These were common ideals and mottos shared by many families and individuals.

We tried hard to live by those words: creating different behaviors, philosophies, and attitudes, even attempting to copy our role models who had seemingly conquered their heart's desire. But, year after year of growing up, out and older, we saw ourselves, not becoming an astronaut, or valedictorian, not an opera singer or first prize winner, but accepting instead, *second* place, *almost* there, and *"maybe tomorrow"* along with that old favorite: *"we'll see."* It was not because we didn't try; we did try and tried hard, many times, sometimes over and over again. But it seems something always got in the way: bad breaks, bad luck, poor timing, health problems, finances, and/or, the kids.

What happened to the dreams? What did we do with them? We were busy going, coming, being and doing, otherwise known as "living," and in so doing we buried the hurt, the disappointment and the sadness that goes along with any unresolved and unhappy event. It became too easy to stuff them away in some hidden corner of our psyche, our deep inner self, that we could almost forget their existence. It never really worked, however, 'cause just when you think everything is going along fine, that old familiar, and unwanted gnawing starts in your belly and creeps its way up to remind you – it's waiting, patiently; your unfinished goals and yearnings want your attention. They want you to deal with them and until you do, they will refuse to leave. In counseling, those sleeping goals are commonly referred to as "unfinished business." In other words, those pieces and bits of unhappiness just want to be recognized and not ignored. Ignoring them makes them grow larger and out of proportion with the rest of your life.

There are a few theories that suggest that folks who avoid facing their sad side and old unfinished issues are prone to frequent changes of location, moving from one house to another, or to one state to another, or frequently changing jobs or marital partners, heavy use of recreational drugs or in general, may have acquired a high need of pleasure satisfaction.

Some people grow impatient or irritable after years of bumping into their tired and weary dreams and pretending they don't exist, pretending they're not painful. Eventually, some of us may find some guidance from talking with a counselor about our buried issues and/or using the endless supply of self-help books found on-line, in libraries and book stores. Learning a new way of looking at our past is helpful, such as: "*I never made it as an airline pilot and I'll always be miserable about that.*" A healthier way of looking at that failure is: "*even though I didn't make it as* a *pilot and maybe I didn't give it my best shot, doesn't mean I'll live with guilt and sadness for the rest of my life. Some of the sadness is real, things like that happen in life, but I can accept that and live with it. I'll never be happy about it, but I don't have to be miserable. After all, I'm not perfect."* Facing ourselves can be such a relief and rarely, is the outcome as traumatic or fearful as we anticipated.

In fact, the outcome usually brings a sense of a more comfortable you........ ready to join the elves and gnomes and slide down the silvery moonbeams.......and that's what I like to do........... "When Dreams Don't Come True."

Summers to Remember

I will not do it. I simply will not pull out the plug that corks the unending vault marked "memories." Once you do, it opens up, spills over and what you get is a vast amount of dribbling of "when I was a kid we did this and that and pretty soon you hear that we ALL did this and that, and why should it become meaningful because we all experienced the same behavior?? Why? I think the answer is that we find comfort in sameness. If we've all "been there, done that, saw that," and apparently "you" and others survived "all that," then there's a good chance "I" might too. When we find comfort in similar behaviors, then it confirms our identity. It says I have behaved the same way you did. We behaved alike, therefore; we're ok, we're sane, we've got it together.

Remembering our past is not only confirming a good memory, as it is assurance our behaviors were within the normal range. If the other kids didn't get into trouble, then most likely we didn't either. Kids played all kinds of games that copied one another, that imitated each other and should you dare to radically differ from your sibs or playmates, and not play the game according to the proper rules, then you pay the consequence of ridicule or teasing. We can't stand those who differ from us, who dress differently or speak differently. Raised by Danish immigrants, I bore the embarrassment and shame of being different. My parents spoke with a noticeable accent and it was not unusual for my little playmates, having been introduced to them, to make fun of their strange ways.

On the other hand: "double dip ice-cream cone, one scoop

vanilla, the other chocolate, dripping down on your hand no matter how fast you lick it." That's a memory - clear, concise. It's ice cold and cools off the whole inside of your mouth. Ridicule, teasing, making fun of a different language, style of dress, kind of play, kind of worship is also remembered on a hot summer day. Warm, wet tears blinding the vision and field of play, make it harder to strike the ball. Yes, kids can be cruel, but isn't it about time we stop using and relying upon that worn-out cliché?

Summer camp – send the little darlin's away to a two week Girl Scout camp so they can learn how to swim, socialize and bake berry pies. Hah! Not necessarily so! At my first camp experience, I was only ten years old and couldn't even float. Finally, on swim instruction day, the counselor actually got into the water with me, (they didn't seem to like to do that very often), grabbed the back straps of my suit as she plunked me into the water and sweetly said, "Now swim, damnit, swim!" I did. I dog-paddled as fast as I could to get away from her. I didn't know for sure what she was going to do to me next!!

The next day was mixed group swim, meaning that the Boy Scouts came over for swim and lunch. A period entitled "free swim" meant you could swim any stroke you wanted. During a brief period, about ten of us girls were jumping and cutely frolicking about in waist deep water as approximately ten-twelve boys were sitting and posing in manly postures on the beach, watching the girls in the water. We girls came up with a ravishing idea! All together. We would hold hands, kick, splash and run, while laughing our most beautiful smile, towards the sand. We were sure without saying so that every boy on the beach would fall madly in love with us. Now I happened to be wearing an old two piece, familiar suit, that I knew from experience how it behaved when I was under the water. If I stood up quickly, the water pressure would pull the top down. So, I was going to outsmart the suit, right? As we jumped up high from the waves I quickly pulled the top *up* so the water wouldn't pull it down! How was I to know that I could pull the suit top up *too far?* I saw ten-twelve young boys simultaneously drop their lower jaws, aghast, followed by thunderous uproar of laughing, non-stop-non-stop-non-stop- I died. Well, at least, I tried to, but I was not able to stay underwater long enough, and besides, I was starting to shiver and dinner was served.

The next camp day offered its own special challenge. We were instructed to pick cherries for pies for dinner. I always walked barefoot and cherry picking time was no exception. Ignoring advice from a counselor, I set out to pick my quota, headed towards the cherry trees, stepped forward towards the base of a tree that housed a nest of wasps, upon which I firmly planted one foot and then the other. The next day, with my swollen feet wrapped in bandages, I spent sitting on the beach reading my Nancy Drew mysteries. "Not bad", said I to myself. At least I don't have to practice the dog paddle and no opportunity to embarrass myself in front of all the young boys in the whole wide world.

If we absolutely must indulge in typical memory lane, then let's throw in the next examples and get it over with: getting dad to get the small tables out and set them up with our chairs on a busy neighborhood street corner. We kids make the lemonade (mom inspects and approves), and we get rich in one afternoon.

(Most of our customers are our neighbors, and I think that's why they pay us so much).

Now, the next story is sure to provoke an eye roller of every listener. (That's when the eyes of the listener look up at the ceiling and then focus from side to side, meaning, ("Oh, Lord, help me, not again!!") The lemonade money pays for our movie tickets the next hot afternoon. We ride the hot bus, get to the movie theater, buy our ticket and walk into a frigid movie house and settle in for a double feature and cold fingers and toes. Pure heaven! We had plenty of time to cool off, 'cause as you must know by now, we sat through several cartoons, a weekly short adventure thriller, like the "Perils of Pauline," RKO Pathe News and two *(two)* full length films. Oh, I forgot - previews of coming films.

In the places I have just visited in my mind's eye, air-conditioning was mostly used in hospitals, department stores, and some places of business. Life in the "good old summertime" was frequently lived outside as most families did not have air-conditioning, but relied on floor or table fans. Hopefully, after a fun picnic in your backyard of hot dogs from the charcoal grill, you would enjoy a cooling breeze in the evening on the front stoop. (Do you know what a "stoop" is)?

Seems to me that little kids were somewhat oblivious to the weather of the day. They just didn't pause in their games and say: "Gee, it sure is hot today, isn't it?"

"Yeah, what's the temp?" We were too busy doing all the fun things kids do on a hot summer day, than to pay attention to temperature and humidity.

Remembering is fun. And I still love ice-cream and hot dogs, but no AC!?? When it's 95 degrees???? That's just not my cup of tea – unless it's *iced* tea, that is, served up with a big dose of "the good ole days," in the coolest room of an air-conditioned home…..and just let me tell you how we could go the movies, (double feature, news, serials and cartoons), round trip bus ride and a coke - and all for only a quarter!!! Let me tell you!! Again! Again! And Again!!

Not an Ordinary Clock

I am not an ordinary clock. I don't stand on the floor and chime like a grandfather clock who tells his endless tale at midnight nor do I reside in a wealthy district in a church bell tower with brass, hand forged bells adorning a clock that peels across the heather blooming over the moors. I'm sure I must have some distant family in London as there are almost more clocks and tower clocks (aside from Big Ben) than there are English chaps and their mums. I'm not really as ornate and important as my cousins in the financial district of New York City, who proclaim the daily gong of the stock market opening and closing to the anxiously awaiting townsfolk. I must say I'm not quite sure I would want that responsibility, which, at times, or so I'm told, can be quite grim. Oh, I'm sorry, I've become rather sidetracked. You probably would like to know where I live. I'll tell you the full story in a little moment, but for now let me say, I adorn the wall of a sweet old fashioned cottage. I don't take up the entire wall, but I'm not tiny either. I am a good sturdy time piece, made of teak, with a face of Roman numerals and easy to read. I may be plain, but I'm told I'm handsome with a sturdy look about me. I announce the hour and the half hour with two distinct notes; the second note lower and softer than the first. While the first note has a heavier and louder accent, like: CUC – koo. On the full hour, I cuckoo the number of corresponding hours, while on the half hour, I only cuckoo once. I have received loving and caring attention from my owners for many years. I am a windup clock, which means if there's a cessation of electric power, I just keep right on ticking. Of more importance, my owners, my master and his family and I have an interdependent relationship. They are dependent upon me for the correct time and I am dependent upon them for the wherewithal to deliver the time (as long as they wind me). It is usually the master of the house who does so. He is fastidious about his commitment, and I respect him for that quality as well as other admirable traits he possesses. After all, where would I be if he forgot about me?

I am different from other clocks in this area, however. In fact, you might say I am different in several ways. I am referred to as a "cuckoo clock," but I have no cuckoo bird that makes an appearance to sound the time. No door opens to welcome any bird, nor little dancing folks twirling about.(I sound the time from within my house, not outside). Moreover, I was not made in the Black Forest area in Germany from whence most cuckoos originated. I was made in Denmark a long time ago, coming from a land of level geography, farmland and seas. I am not ornate with many flourishes, but of simple, calm design, pleasing and restful to the eye. No matter, for I believe that does not make me any less a cuckoo than the fancier kind. While we're defining this and that, I'm not sure why the word "cuckoo" is used to describe one who is silly or foolish, when it is the cuckoo bird who lays her eggs in the nests of other birds to hatch. Hm - - maybe not so silly...

I remember sounds and sights of Copenhagen and Elsinore: village cobblestone streets, houses close, and some adjacent to one another with red and yellow flowers cascading from window boxes and a broom resting by each doorstep for the morning sweep smells of the oceans and seas drifting across the harbors and into town on the wings, and cawing of gulls swooping everywhere in the sunlight, and the sweet odors of warm bread and pastries from the early morning bakeries, eaten on a wooden bench next to a cart filled with all kinds of cheese. It was my home. I belonged to a schoolmaster, a principal really, of a well-known school and when his brother told him of his intent to travel to America, he gave him a gift of me. I was, initially, somewhat sad to learn of our pending departure (his brother and me), but I had been so well cared for, I was not fearful of our adventure. I was fortunate that I will always have the memories of white lace caps, colorful skirts swirling to folk dances, blonde hair blue-eyed kindly people named Eric, Peter or, of course, King Christian, riding in his royal carriage. I realize that the feelings of loss will be minimal for I will be cared for by a Danish gentleman and his family. I have been owned by members of his family ever since I was created, approximately fifty years ago.

I cuckoo in Danish, which sounds very much like an English cuckoo. However, we, the family of clocks may be unusual as we do not mind speaking a variety of languages or being different from one another. We do not necessarily revere sameness and alikeness. We do believe that we have some special abilities of communication and caring among ourselves, but we generally keep this to ourselves. We may speak the language of our birth, but we are also able to speak a universal tongue, even understanding our keepers. I can't explain why except that's how we were made. While I'm attempting to describe us, I should mention that among the values we honor, are: consistency, perseverance, and determination; rather important for clocks, don't you think?

Lastly, we value those whom we serve as well as honoring

each other; and consider ourselves to be a compassionate community, no matter where we live.

I have serviced my family for many years and have become very attached to them. For instance, would you believe that I hear all, see all and remember all that occurs in our house? So it must be if I am to be a valuable time keeper.

The life of a clock can be exciting, joyful, quiet or sad, depending upon the activities and routines of its owners. Most folks probably think we just reside in our assigned station, half dozing and barely coming to life until it's time to cuckoo. There were certainly times when I didn't feel like announcing the hour; times when my master's wife was awfully ill or when the young master's fiancée left him. Do you really think I felt good piercing the silence throughout a house laden with sadness, with a silly, repetitive "cuckoo" echoing through the darkened rooms? I didn't. But then, I would look forward to the return of gay times again and they would always return, thank heaven for that. How can I ever forget the dancing and laughing and singing? Those are the times really worth chiming about. Once in a while, the entire family would go away on a vacation. I would be left alone. Those times were hard for me and I just slept a lot, but, I kept sounding the hour and the half hour, even though there was no one there to hear but me.

Recently, our special powers of communication became quite necessary. Lately, I've heard clocks talk about strangers who have been heard or seen in our neighborhood. It's those gigantic grandfather clocks that stand five to six feet tall that resounded the news and when they chime out a message, other clocks can hear it for miles around. They warned us to be on guard, not that we needed to be warned, because we are always looking out for our family. Nonetheless, warnings echoed across the hills of thefts that had been occurring late at night in nearby villages. All of us became especially vigilant, staying awake and alert later than usual.

Then, just as they warned, it happened. It was during the winter, around two a.m. and from my position I could see the softly falling snow through the double doors to the patio. A nearby light brightly lit the area, except for one corner of the doors, where the building cast a shadow. I was watching the snow when it appeared as though the shadow started to move, and as I continued to look at it, it slowly moved towards the door handle. Then I could see a shadowy hand on the door latch, and it began trying to open the door. Of course, I didn't worry because we have an alarm system, and I knew the minute they might open the door, the sirens would scream and also notify the police. But it didn't. Someone opened the door and nothing happened. My master and the family must have forgotten to set the alarm! Someone was slowly and carefully stepping into the house. Something had to be done *now!* Horrified, I realized the time was not on or half past the hour, it was in-between, on the quarter hour - at a time when I have never cuckooed, ever! In spite of the slim chance I would be able to sound any type of alarm, I gathered all the strength I could muster and as loudly and as fast as I could, I started to *cuckoo cuckoo cuckoo cuckoo* over and over again. My cries must have been heard, at least by some of the gigantic grandfather clocks for they started to sound their chimes, so many of them and at the same time that you could hear them throughout the entire village and it was *magnificent*. For every kind of clock now joined in and was ringing out together to save my little family. It worked. My master bounded out of bed, a police car on patrol nearby rushed to our house, and the burglar was apprehended. My master admitted to the sheriff that he must have neglected to turn on the alarm and the officer said, "Well, you folks must have some sort of alarm system here, because it sounds like someone is looking out for you. Pretty nice how you take care of one another. And clocks of every kind.

Then I really felt goodbecause I heard my master say to his wife, "You know this is just a notion that I have, but if I didn't know better, I'd say that it was our very own cuckoo clock who is the hero of the day."

When I heard that, I burst with pride and sent out one of our silent chime/cuckoo messages to all, that said, "Thank you to cuckoos and clocks of every kind, everywhere, whether English, Danish, from Elsinore, Ireland or New York. May we always chime for one another, no matter what the time."

The Big Three

NO – I don't mean the "big three" automotive companies. I'm talking about The Pumpkin, the Turkey and the Tree!! Meaning the big three r-e-a-l-l-y-big events, (that by the time you read this), are: one will have passed, one will be here and the last is waiting in the wings. I'm talking about Halloween, Thanksgiving and Christmas.

I don't know about you, but it seems I'm having a harder time keeping up with the even fewer demands of each holiday. How can that possibly be when now, in retirement, an invitation for an appetizer and drink is sufficient for most folks. The standards and the demands have changed drastically. But I bet, that many of you, like me, wonder how we possibly "did it all," especially when we were gainfully employed. How did I maintain my "gainful employment"(whether it was inside the home or outside of the home), while tearing around to get ready for Halloween. W-Mart for costumes, (except for the Superman costume which I made), pumpkins, candy by the armfuls, apples and pennies. If I got extra lucky, I found myself hosting the neighborhood costume party including pumpkin cookies and hot dogs dressed up like scarecrows, according to the recipe in Woman's magazine which you had better follow in order to rank right up there with all the other frenzied mothers.

I was sitting on our deck in the shadows of the late afternoon sun, remembering those times of younger days, and feeling drowsy, looking at our pumpkin patch groaning under the weight of our plump-bellied orange ladies, all wearing green caps when, "Can my pumpkin have the mean face, this year,

Daddy? Last time you said if mine had the smiley face, then this year Bobby could do the smiley face and mine would be mean and scary. Right? Huh?"

I looked around the deck and back yard and saw no one. The childlike voice (which sounded like mine) must have been the cool breeze rustling through the last, crisp autumn leaves that are too stubborn to let go; or, maybe I dozed off for a few minutes.

"OK, darling, you're right, I remember saying that. I did promise."

"Ah-h Dad, I don't want to do a pretty cute face. My pumpkin should look mean.......

"Well, I did promise Susie,...."

"Oh, mother, please," maybe we could both do a mean one..."

I seemed to "wake up" and realize I was leaning back, rocking on our porch swing and caught myself listening to what must have been a wide-awake dream of a pumpkin decorating session with our children when they were little. We called it a "decorating session" because we celebrated the autumn and harvest aspects of Halloween, omitting the witches and goblins. We put colored leaves into scrapbooks, read or made up stories about the Pilgrims and Indians, made apple sauce and sweet potato pies and of course, we sang our favorite harvest songs for both autumn and Thanksgiving:

"Come ye thankful people, come: Sing the song of harvest time;
All is safely gathered in, 'er the winter storms begin..." Or –
" We gather together to ask the Lord's blessings,
He hastens and chastens to his will to make known....."

I think there are some times, more than others, when images of the kids, sounds of the kids or just the sense in the air when they were nearby, when you're missing them so much that you just have to DO something. So I called John and said, "Why don't we carve one of those huge pumpkins, light it tonight and put it on our front stoop? I know it won't really bring us nearer to them, but maybe it will bring us closer." (We also agreed that carving a pumpkin, maybe just this once, would be ok).

Assisted living is really a wise thing to do, so, anticipating our needs in the future, we signed up for it the other day. Change is always hard, but we can do it. We're having the turkey dinner by ourselves this year; it's really too far to drive north with the threat of snowstorms. As John and I were carving the turkey and testing the trimmings, I couldn't help but recall scenes from our Thanksgiving dinner with the kids, just prior to our trip to the south:

"Oh, Grandma, look at the snow coming down. Will it be like that where you're going, to Tennessee?".....and "Grandma," asked Jennifer, "can I pull the wishbone with you?"

"Of course," I said" and "Grandma, when you get through going to retirement tomorrow morning, will you come over to my house and play with me?" (I don't think she saw my tears).

The "Big Three" are here again, and I'm cozy on our deck which is now enclosed from the elements. I'm curled up under a family hand-made quilt, sipping a cup of tea, and watching the snow flakes drift down on my girls chattering away in the pumpkin patch, their little green hats slightly askew. Watching the snow brought back scenes of presents, busy shopping days, cards to write, cookies to bake, candles and decorations, memories that return; some with a sigh of relief, others with that special sigh that I call "the missing sigh" along with visions of the glowing blue, green and red lights upon a soft needle fir tree.

Now, our tree gets smaller and smaller with each passing holiday. It used to be six feet tall, laden with decorations and John would carry it to the basement, cover it until it made its appearance the next year. Gradually, as we aged and the trees got heavier, we finally settled for a table tree. Taking in our warm surroundings while sitting in front of our tree and fireplace, I gratefully assumed I was as content as I was going to be, when we heard Christmas caroling at our front door. My tears started before John could even open the door, for I'd know the voices of our children and grandchildren anywhere!

"Here We Come A-caroling, among the leaves so green – "Merry Christmas Gramps!" "Oh, what a wonderful surprise and Merry Christmas," we cried, as we almost fell into one another's arms, hugging and kissing and crying. We had our pumpkins, we had our turkey, we have our tree, and now the best of all – we have each other.

I'll Be Loving You, Always

Charlie and Emma sat on the back porch talking about the wonderful times they had during the past three days wIth their son, Eric, daughter-in-law, Susan and two granddaughters, Jane and Jenny. They had arrived for a surprise visit to celebrate Charlie's and Emma's 45th wedding anniversary. It had been two years since they had retired, moving to a semi-warmer climate which they were enjoying, except it usually took a full day's trip by car to visit one another. Visits were getting further and further apart, but as most of the senior folks say, "That's to be expected, they've got their own lives to live."

They celebrated their anniversary by going out to dinner, plus prepared a feast on the actual day of their wedding. They renewed their ties and closeness, initially, by playing some board games, followed by laughing at old photo albums, catching up on current happenings and all washed down with plenty of coke and chips. As far as Charlie and Emma were concerned, that would have more than satisfied any expectations they might have had as a memento of the occasion.

"Wasn't it fantastic?" Emma asked. "Just being with them would have been enough, but how are we ever going to handle and get used to all those machines and gadgets they showered upon us? I don't even remember the names of most of them, let alone how we'll ever learn to use them all."

"Well, Emma," Charlie reminded her, Eric did introduce us to that nice fellow who lives right here in our community who agreed to drop over for a half- hour or so, a few times a week, if necessary, to help us out at least until we feel a little more comfortable with all of it."

"He did seem quite pleasant," Emma agreed, "and I'm certainly glad Eric gave him an extra list of the machines they gave to us. He did say he wanted us to start reading all the booklets that came with everything and I guess we had better get started."

"Right," Charlie replied. "I think I'll retire now and take this booklet about a 'cell phone' to bed with me and see what it has to say. We have got to be the only two people in the world who do not own one. I know our kids must think we're terribly old fashioned and 'behind the times,' but honestly, I'm not sure they realize that when we were in grade school and high school we simply did not have any computers. Maybe they were available in corporations and the business world, but for sure, not to kids or the average household," explained Charlie. "You know, Em, I sound like it's kind of important to me that our brood understands where we're coming from - and on second thought, I guess it is."

"Charlie, I agree completely, but I find it's awfully hard to use any tool when I don't understand the reason for its use. Oh, sure, I realize the benefits of instant communication and comfort in knowing the family's whereabouts quickly, but will you explain how the transition was made from the corner phone booth, enclosed in glass, (with a door, even, for extra privacy) to people everywhere now willing to share the most intimate private matters of their lives, either on the bus, the restaurant, the rest rooms, any waiting line - *heavens - just about anywhere!* - ? Honestly, there are times I feel absolutely embarrassed to overhear the woman next to me in the grocery check-out line is getting divorced in two days. I do not want to know that; I have enough to handle in my own life, let alone her problems."

"Goodness," Emma exclaimed, "I did not mean to get carried away about cell phones. I was going to mention how I think CEO's of corporations are hoodwinking their labor force into believing they are so vital and indispensable, they need to carry a communication gadget, (whatever its called) 24/7 so as to be available *to work longer and extra hours!* I'm no expert on this issue and how do I know? Maybe the employees are compensated for such availability."

Looking a little sheepish, Emma admitted, "Bet you're glad I didn't get into the hoodwinking issue. I didn't know that word was still around!"

"Em, most of the time, I think I have you all figured out and then there are times I think, whoops, I'd better watch myself – this gal has something to say, which I enjoy hearing and I love the word "hoodwinked,' You go on as long as you like."

Charlie continued: "Earlier, I mentioned my concern about our kids thinking we're 'behind times' and sure, no doubt that's true, but I recall whatever time we had after full-time work, we both spent between 2 and 4 years in night school, you, to carve out a new career for yourself and me, for job development, so both of us could deposit funds for the family upkeep and higher education. I really don't think there was a leftover minute for developing computer skills."

"Maybe kids shouldn't be expected to understand parental behaviors. If there are any expectations here, it's *us who were expected to do our best for our children.* Guess that's why you so often hear the seniors, in their effort to gather some appreciation for whatever it was they were able to do, say, '*When I was your age. I......beepity, beep.'* There's not a 5 year old child or a 50 year old (adult) child who will understand that, until, perhaps, *they* become the senior."

"In support of what you're saying, Charlie, one of my favorite Mark "Twain-isms' is: "when I was 17 my father was the most ignorant man I'd ever known . . . by the time I was 21 he was the smartest."

"Mark Twain usually says it all, doesn't he? Most of the phrases I've read along those lines concur that the older the child becomes, the smarter the parents become. I'm not so sure, Em, that our kids see us that way."

"Oh, I'm sure they understand," Emma said, hopefully, "and I'm sure they'll understand we don't learn as fast as we used to. Oh my, I sure hope it isn't true what they say about senior folks."

"And what would that be, Em,?" asked Charlie.

"Oh, some crude saying about not being able to teach old birds' new tricks, or something like that..."Emma responded.

"There may be some truth to that," Charlie agreed, "but I'm sure our kids don't think that about us, mainly because, *we're not old! Right?"*

"*Right!*" Emma responded.

"Charlie, I think we've been chatting too long, which is probably a symptom of our procrastination. I had better get serious now. Eric advised me to start with something uncomplicated," Emma explained, "like playing these small records that look something like our old 45's. That's a beautiful piece of furniture they had delivered and that's where we put these small records when we play them. I'll let you know tomorrow if I learn about it."

"Right, Emma, just don't get so smart you'll forget to make my breakfast in the morning. We don't need a gadget for that, do we?" Charlie teased.

"Oh, Charlie, sleep tight, darling."

The next few weeks Emma and Charlie read their booklets and literature and began to practice using their new "gadgets." They became acquainted with most of the basic operations, but put off reading about the more complicated instructions regarding their Direct HD Satellite Television and recording and/or playing a DVD movie, until they became more comfortable with what they had learned thus far. Charlie was beginning to operate the CD's and Emma was sending a few emails and even though their progress wasn't speedy, they were beginning to understand some of the basics.

"Boy," Charlie would say, "sure wish that Eric lived closer by us and he would be able to pop over and straighten us out on all this stuff. It's great to have but...."

" *BEEP …BEEP…BEEP…*" holy cow, what's that? Lately, I'm getting beeped from all over the house. There goes another one and I'm not sure if it's a low battery on the cell phone… or what it is, maybe, it's…"

"Maybe," interrupted Emma, 'the new toaster convection counter oven is telling us it's ready," ….

"Did you turn on the oven, Em?"

"Oh, I'm not real sure if I did or not. I know I put some clothes in the dryer and maybe that's where the beep sound is coming from. Honestly, I can't keep track of all the different sounds anymore," Emma complained.

"God Bless America," suddenly rang out by a full choir from the direction of the dining room.

"Heavens to Betsy," cried Emma, "did I leave something on again? Where in the world is the music coming from?"

"I do believe," Charlie informed his wife, "that's our new cell phone and whenever someone calls, it's supposed to play that song."

"Well, I didn't know about that," Emma admitted. "Am I supposed to stand by it and sing 'God Bless America' with it - - or do I pick it up first and then sing along with it?"

"Em, here's what you do. You walk over to the phone, read the screen next to it to see who's calling and then….."

"What in tarnation are you talking about? I stand over it and without picking it up, I ask it who's calling?" questioned Emma.

"No, not exactly. You see, this device is called "caller ID" and it spells out the name of the person calling so you can decide whether or not you want to speak with that person, or not, and if you don't, just let the answering machine take a message."

"Well, I think that's terrible. Here, some person is nice enough to give you a call and first of all, we take all the surprise out of it. I believe that when a phone rings, you should pick it up and say 'Hello,' and that's how you discover whose calling. I never heard of such a thing," Emma complained.

"I understand, Em. This way it just gives you the option," Charlie explained.

Beginning to feel a little bit overwhelmed, Emma asked, "Charlie, why don't I make us a cup of tea?"

And I'll fix the toast," offered Charlie. While getting the cups out for the tea, the microwave beeped its readiness four times, the new toaster three times and the toaster oven gave five beeps, shortly followed by Charlie's alarm wrist watch which dings three times letting the wearer know that it's time for the next dose of pills and if that wasn't enough, their cuckoo clock started to cuckoo nine times. Emma started to cry just as the wind chimes outside their deck door started swinging on a new breeze: "dingdongdingdumding........"

"Oh, that's it, Charlie, maybe I'm the cuckoo one and not the clock. The other day I got so frustrated when I wanted to play some of our old love songs and I couldn't get those little disc things into the machine, I wanted to watch my favorite soap on TV and couldn't find the right channel number and then went to answer the phone and it was the dishwasher ending its cycle, which sounds just like the new phone. I'm surprised I didn't take a glass out of the dishwasher and put it to my ear and say 'Hello?' I give up, Charlie, I just give up!"

"Now Em, let's just relax here and give ourselves a little break. We have been working pretty hard on all this and trying to learn it all at the same time. Just give me a little time to think," and pausing for a moment, Charlie said, "I know. Why don't you get all prettied up this Friday night and I'll treat you for a surprise. How does that sound?"

"Charlie, that may be just what I need."

Charlie and Emma met in their living room in the early evening at the pre-arranged time the next Friday, dressed in their semi-formal clothes. It seemed to Emma that Charlie had been busier than usual around the house and running miscellaneous errands, as well. Emma couldn't help but wonder what Charlie was planning and arranging. Charlie smiled as he handed Emma a white florist box which she opened and smiled right back for it contained the most beautiful perfumed gardenia along with a white orchid. "Oh, Charlie! You shouldn't have, but I'm so glad you did."

Charlie, holding out his arm, said: "Emma, you look simply ravishing. "Right this way, my dear."

Much to Emma's surprise, Charlie led her to their finished basement, where he had turned down the lights, had placed candles everywhere, set up a corner with their old TV with one of Emma's favorite chairs nearby and a small table to hold her tea cup with the latest TV guide with which Emma was familiar. He had also brought in bouquets of flowers, trays of appetizers and pretty drinks situated on a coffee table in front of a sofa, all complimented by a gentle fire in the fireplace. Charlie took Emma's hand and led her over to their old record player, where he handed her a 33 and 1/3 record and asked her to pick out her favorite tune and when she did, she handed it to him, he put it on and it began to play their favorite song: "I'll Be Loving You, Always." And with that, Charlie gracefully waltzed his love across the floor.

"Oh, Charlie, you are so wonderful."

"We don't need anything, but each other, Em, and after we take another little break, we'll happily revisit all those wonderful marvels our son gave to us. We'll surprise the whole family and us and with a little more time, we'll become experts and just come down here to hear some of the real old songs and have a little dance or two."

"In the mean time, in between time, may I have another waltz with my fair lady?"

"Oh, Charlie, I love you."

"And I love you, Em, *always*"

Little Kids Get Scared

I don't tell anyone 'cause
I don't want to be called a sissy,
But sometimes I get scared
Like when that big kid at school
Dared me and my dad said, "Dare him back,"
But I was too scared to, so I ran.
I didn't tell my dad that I ran.

One time when I was walking home from school
A mean dog started to chase me
Barking, snarling and when he grabbed my pant leg
I could feel his hot breath. His owner finally
Called him, but boy, was I scared.
After that I crossed the street whenever
I got near his house.

Last week when I was talking with some guys
Mary Lou came over and put her hand into mine;
I couldn't believe it cause it made me feel
Funny and weird all over and so scared
I didn't know what to do next.
The guys laughed.

Last night I lay in my bed
With the covers pulled up over my head.
My mom and dad were yelling real loud
At each other.
They sometimes do that
When they drink or smoke and that
Makes me more scared than I was of the big kid,
The mean dog or Mary Lou.

Off to School

Where the swing set was –
that's where they played.
I would watch them
as the late afternoon sun
faded into quiet sleepy shade.
They were so little then;
where have they gone?
They are so grown now,
Did we ever say goodbye?

I only know they're not here anymore
and that's as it should be,
or so says my mind, but not my heart;
for they left their laughter behind
that echoes where they played,
drifting on a breeze
from the back of the yard.

They jumped, they hopped, and giggled,
They turned the mornings
into pink, lavender and gold.
They implored the heavens
and the heavens responded
with melodies I still hear
in my minds quiet mode;
when the late afternoon sun
faded into sleepy shade,
where the swing set was –
the place where they once played.

Rain

Rain weeps when it falls in the morning. Maybe it's confused and unsure how long it will fall, or whether it will sprinkle or pour. Will there be winds with the rain, or will it find its own way to the succulent earth? Sometimes a morning rain becomes an all day rain – a rain that doesn't catch its breath or rest for a minute or two; just keeps coming down, steadily, on and on. I wonder if rain ever feels sad, like on a motionless morning, before my mind engages and begins the day. I might start gathering old sorrows that begin creeping in, uninvited, mingling tear drops with rain drops, but not for long, for the sun is thinking about shining and like a spoiled child, it usually gets its way.

Afternoon rain is heavy; sometimes it takes all morning for rain to fill up a cloud and when it finally starts to pour, it brings that sweet, heavy, thick air, bursting with the strong, wet smell of the earth and I hear little voices singing and giggling from their hiding place under the front porch: "It's raining, it's pouring, the old man is snoring……" and then how *glorious – a rainbow!* The thunder will make the announcement, clear the stage and there in red, orange, yellow, green, blue and violet arches is one of natures' triumphs! What could be better? Of course! A double rainbow! Now, that's the tour de force!!

When I was a real little kid, I loved rain and I think rain loves little kids. Rain makes jumping puddles for kids stomping and splashing and getting their friends all wet - because he got me first and it wasn't my fault – it was the rain.

One time, though, I think rain must have been angry with me because it came down hard, on my outdoor birthday party. It happened so fast we didn't have time to get the cake indoors. We all got wet and just laughed and danced around the picnic table, singing and eating wet frosting that our fingers scooped up from my wet cake.

I remember a time when my parents and two sisters and I were sitting outside on our lounge chairs, enjoying the sun and chatting, when it gradually started to rain. We were in our back yard and not very far from the door to the house. I don't know how to explain it, but without a word or a signal, all of us apparently decided to completely ignore the rain and carry on our conversation as though nothing was happening. The rain increased , harder, faster, splattering, pouring, soaking our clothes, our hair, everywhere and everything; there we sat, calm, composed, unemotional and engaging in the most interesting of conversations until one of us simply couldn't hold back the laughter any longer….. and then, we thought we'd never catch our breath from all the laughing.

There were many night times when rain came to call. Sometimes I would feel lonely at night and lie in my bed alone and in the dark, and the rain would start to fall, slowly, "pit pat - pit pat - pit pat" at first and then the thunder, far away, would begin to clear its throat, almost politely, announcing its intention of "coming to call," as folks used to say long ago, "just a short visit, is all." I would slip further down between the covers, preparing for the concert soon to begin, but I would leave my ears half poking out because no matter how loud and rambunctious it got, I still didn't want to miss how the rain sounds as it leaves the clouds in heaven and tumbles to the earth below.

By the way, do you know how hot it can get when you're under the covers, and you can't come out because the thunder's too loud, and you're too scared to take the covers away? So, you wait until the thunder gets softer and starts to go away, then you can lie in bed and listen to the rain, little by little, sing its last song of the storm. Thank you, rain, for sleeping with me and keeping me company. Thank you for singing your song and if you want, you can stay the whole night long.

Little Kids' Tall Tales

The other day after school
My mom forgot to pick me up
So I went out into the street to look for her
And got hit by a school bus
Well, not really, but she was late.

My mom smokes cigarettes
She thinks I don't know about it
'cause she hides them on top of the refrigerator
Where we can't see them, but I know they're there.
I just made that up, but grandma sure looked surprised
When I told her.

I have a new baby sister
She just showed up, all of a sudden out of nowhere.
I guess she's going to live with me.
Tomorrow when she gets bigger
I'll be able to play with her.
She's real cute; even as cute as me.

My grandma has a goody drawer
That we can open and have anything we want.
One time she made our lunch before she went shopping
But when she was gone grandpa let us eat
Chocolate cookies and milk instead.
Grandma didn't even get mad.

We like to stay at our gramps house
Grandma sings to us and reads stories

Once Upon a Time

Grandpa chases us and then we chase him
We go for walks in the woods and watch kiddie movies
We all like each other a lot.

One day we played cowboys and Indians
We had so much fun.
Then they said goodbye 'cause
They were leaving in the morning
To retire in Florida, so we said:
"When you get through retiring in Florida tomorrow,
Will you come over and play with us?"

Little Kids' Shoes

When I was real little I wore tiny shoes
That mom painted gold and put on the
TV set and when I asked her why
She just smiled and then cried.

I liked my patent leather tap dancing shoes
The best you could hear me coming and when
I danced in a recital I wouldn't get off the stage
I liked it so much I stayed awake all night.

After kindergarten when I was grown up
And when it stopped snowing I didn't have
To wear snowpants just only my white boots.
I loved my white boots.

I wanted lots of shoes I didn't get
Like moccasins that Indians wear
Or kitty slippers or red shoes I did get bunny
Slippers sneakers for gym and leftovers
They are my sister's old shoes.

Now I'm wearing white shoes with lace and pearls
'cause my sister says I'm her flower girl
As I sprinkle daisies in front of her wedding gown
I wonder: will the shoes she's wearing today
Be my hand-me-downs tomorrow?

Listen to the Falling Snow

Winter is polite when it first arrives
Hidden inside drifting clouds about to let go
Of a snowfall of silence; snowflakes floating dreamily
Down, fluttering tremulously, to the earth below.
- fluttering tremulously to the earth below.

The silent descent of snow upon a world so quiet
Reaches the ground and layers itself into mounds of tranquil white.
And should the winds begin to howl, the kindergarten teacher will
Beseech her charges to lie down and nap upon their little braided rugs.
- and nap upon their little braided rugs.

However, if Sarah, in the back row, begins to whisper to Billy
The teacher will admonish: "hush, hush, now," and
Should Billy whisper back, the teacher will say:
"Just hush, now, and listen, listen to the falling snow.
- just listen to the falling snow."

Sometimes, when it was too cold or windy to go outside,
Or we were too excited about the new snow,
We would sit by the windowpanes and watch winter paint pictures
Of frosty delicate and lacy ferns, like those asleep down below –
- like those asleep beneath the snow.

Later, when at home, I would wait for the moon to rise
And watch it cast diamonds on the sleeping snow,
For the teacher had said: "there's a full moon tonight,
So, just hush and look at winter's heavenly lights,
- just look at winter's heavenly lights
and listen to the falling snow."

The Weeping Cherry Tree

I am the Weeping Cherry tree standing in the center of our yard.
I am at the height of my bloom and I am magnificent.
I am full of pink and white clusters of buds unfolding and
Soft flowers opening to face a brilliant sun that is bursting with
Light – glorious and warm, soft and golden in a canopy of pristine blue.
The breezes sigh in and out among my branches and I stretch my long
Arms to enfold their caresses while small creatures on wing offer
Lullabies to my splendor; as I welcome them to a safe haven of rest.
This is how it should be. This is how it needs to be, but I know it won't last.
Already I feel my branches beginning to lean towards the spring scented earth,
My treasured petals becoming weaker and beginning to let go of the
Dreams they once nourished of unending blooms, now fading and falling
As tears that trickle into streams and gullies into waiting
Ponds and pools, dreamingly sailing into dark waters of a lagoon;
Remembering when tears were flowers kissed by the sun, flowers
That will return, that will come again, if only I can wait long enough.

January

I don't like January.   Never have. Never will.
It's like the morning after whatever and time to pay the bill.
The caroling has stopped, the singing has ceased,
Leaving the last revelers the remainders of the feast.

January is for leftovers - - leftover pie,
Be it Shepard's or berry or turkey on rye,
It's also for the new love that started in the snow
Of December, now discarded with the mistletoe.

The neighborhood that looked like a fairyland galore
With lights on every shrub and wreaths on every door -
Is now stripped bare, wiped clean, without a clue
That any sled flew over or anyone squeezed down a flue.

The merry shoppers who bought on-line and in stores,
Are lining up and signing on to return their gifts before
It's too late for that size, "Don't have any more around
That'll fit your waist and all those holiday pounds."

The end of last year brought us holidays of fun
During the past four months each had a special one,
But January is like arriving at the ball too late,
Except for day one (and a few famous folks) what's to
celebrate?

Then maybe its time to light the fire and snuggle down
And think about the holidays, so quickly here, then gone.
While we walk in the wonder of the sparkles on the snow
Remembering bright colored lights – wondering -
where did they go?

Time to Take a Nap

Enough is enough! I've sung the praises of the seasons as they danced by; from April arias, May's waltz of the flowers, bittersweet September, to indolent summer and its lusty heat and – I need a break! March is coming! The meanest of all months is almost here. It's harsh and unforgiving; it will cut you no slack or sympathy. If you're not ready to stand up to it, the best thing to do is to get away from it all – take a nap! After all – bears do it! Squirrels do it. Woodchucks and even Marmots do it! So, LET'S *DO IT. WHY NOT TAKE A NAP?*

Naps are good for you; short ones, long ones, whatever kind you like. They're all beneficial. Naps are also convenient. They can be taken any time of the year with longer naps occurring more often during the cold months and you have a choice of whatever sleep state you prefer, from a short shut-eye to a state of hibernation. (Actually, some of our napping would be regarded as a *modified* state of hibernation, also known as one of those vacations where all you want to do is rest and sleep and rest and sleep).....When you stop to think of it, in some ways we're similar to animals in our pre-napping and actual napping behaviors, as follows:

1. Animals incessantly feed and forage during the months close to hibernation, storing the excess nutrients in their body fat. We regard our foraging as an obligation, as well as a responsibility to honor the traditions associated with Thanksgiving and Christmas holidays, even supplying ourselves with ready made rationalizations:" Oh well, *they* say we're supposed to put on five pounds every holiday – everybody does!"

2. Prior to hibernation, animals slow down their activity and

most of their physical movements are focused on foods. Humans do not hibernate as long as animals, but with the onset of colder temperatures, begin to prepare for an altered state by engaging in fewer games of sport, with golf activity slowing down or halting completely. Isn't it about now that the "little woman" attempts to manage her reaction to having hubby at elbow distance by "putting up" the harvest into sterilized glass jars with labels. Again, an example of the focus on food collection, preparation and storing prior to taking a nap.

3. While animals do not assemble in precise exercise groups and stand in well spaced circles or straight lines (except in Disney movies), they do curtail their activity. We seem to alter our motion from speedy-normal to slow-slower by locking gym and pool doors more often during the holiday season; then, shucks, it's not our fault if we can't exercise, so might as well catch 40 winks (or so. Why is it always 40?)

4. Finally, other desires are also put to sleep and a note is pinned to the nightgown that says, "I've got a headache, I'm hibernating, wake me when it's spring," - prompting some weary spouse to mutter, "So what else is new?"

In view of the above, the only thing there is to say is:

March is almost here. Better hurry and get some nap time before it's time to get up! It's cold. It's windy. Pay the dentist and tell the doc he can do without our sorry aching limbs for a month or so and no need to trim the few hairs on top or curl the locks and to everyone else, "We'll put a check in the mail." We've emptied the "honey do" jar, exercised some of the time, played golf a lot of the time and *now is the time – to* cease all the services, the mail and the paper, the catered evening meals, the weekly massages, tennis lessons, eyebrow penciling, and T'aiChi classes, our relaxation therapy and finally, our registration for history lectures of the surrounding five mile radius and any and all classes on how to artfully assemble and glue pieces of special papers into a large book, in six sessions, that used to take us 20 minutes when we were seven years old and called it a "scrapbook." The big difference now, is that for extra monies, our book will have golden letters embossed on the cover that spells "Memories" and it didn't belong to your big sister with some of her leftovers still glued to the pages. Ah well, the cruel fate of leftovers.

Once we fulfill our obligations (and no fair just dropping the dog off at the doggie park, with a note, "Please feed me", it's time to just curl up (or down, whichever you do) and don't even listen to the daffodils trumpeting for attention because the weeds are choking them and learn to ignore and dismiss all the racket and clamor made by buds bursting and forsythia emerging. They're just trying to get our attention and remind us of all the garden work that waits. We may have started our nap a little late in the season, but now it's our turn – we've earned it.

"OK, good night." "Good Night."

Silence More silence.

"I'm really not sleepy," says spouse number one.

"I'm not either. Do you think that maybe we should get a head start on the garden?" questions spouse number two.

"I think we should hurry and beat the deer to the tulip bulbs and get out there right away!" responds spouse one.

"Let's go – we can always nap !!!! Hurry up!!!!"

"I'm right behind you….and later, when we're done, let's go…to the….and after that, ...visit………and then, we can………."

Shortcuts to Serenity

Introduction

I have heard it said that if you're feeling lonely, sad or uptight, you need to lean back, close your eyes and pretend you're in a place that is peaceful, calm and serene. If you just imagine it, (so I'm told) you will begin to feel better. But don't take my word for it. Just read the stories below and perhaps it will work for you. Enjoy your journey.

The Woodland Path

"I know of a path that lazily wanders and meanders through a meadowland laced with white and yellow daises slumbering and swaying in the late afternoon sun while awaiting the song of the wood lark that sings on amber beams of light, streaming down from the tree tops to the earth below.

Here's the path I've been looking for. We'll walk slowly, taking in deep breaths of cool air, as we enjoy the many shapes and colors of flowers in full bloom. It seems as though we have been transported to a rain forest, or a jungle filled with wild dreams of orange striped tiger lilies under polka dot skies. The path becomes surrounded by large dark green leaves, plants of purple and orange, gardens of magenta and turquoise flowers and overhead - deep blue/green feathery branches dip down into pools of reflective sunlight. The earth has a scent that reminds us of opening an old cellar door, left forgotten and undisturbed for too many seasons; where sagging cellar shelves are still laden with old canning jars filled with hopes and tears, now outdated and covered with dust, left in a place where dreams never visit anymore. We quickly leave the thick, dank air for the welcome sight of soft streams of gold filtered light scattering its glittering rays over the exotic foliage,

As we continue to walk, we sense a breeze stirring in the trees, perfumes of wildflowers, the breathtaking assemblage of yellow roses, white orchids, mixed with gigantic bright pink peonies beckoning us to enter further, deeper into the woods and learn of its secrets. If we listen carefully, we begin to notice a faint, constant, whispering from alongside the path, resembling the swishing rustle of layer upon layer of old-fashioned satin petticoats stitched with eyelet laces and velvet ribbons. We discover the whispering emanates from a profusion of thick purple violets intermingled with leaves similar to those of the popular trees who always whisper and rustle when the moon is white in the midnight sky.

We begin to hear sweet melodies coming from on high above the tree branches, weaving in and out, coming closer, when we notice flocks of birds; yellow, light blue, some of soft pink and lavender making their way towards us, fluttering all around us, singing a haunting, yet lilting song.

As if on cue, peacocks of every color imaginable begin to slowly emerge from the foliage, strutting, with heads held high, prancing in and about, making small fluted sounds, haughty and arrogant, dancing as if to show off their arc of multi- one-eyed feathers just for our pleasure. The birds and peacocks appear to be captured in an enchanted land of long ago, an imaginary fantasy place once called Shangri - La; idyllic and remote: a hideaway only for those who share quiet affections and enduring love.

We decide to rest on a soft cushion of moss, lean back, take in a deep breath and just listen…..to the sound of one dewdrop upon a leaf directly above us, as it splashes down to the leaf below. We watch, fascinated, as it fills with more moisture, then becomes so heavy it trickles down again and again, to the next leaf and the next... 'til all the dew drops have become a small rippling pond

> Where sleepy woodland creatures come to rest by its side
> Snuggling down together in the quiet, green glen:
> Says the wide-eyed owl and his soft feathery friends
> Just close your eyes and dream of the dawn,
> Fold your little paws and sleep on and on.

We become mesmerized, surrounded, and engulfed, by our surroundings, blending in and becoming as one.. We are content to stay where we are, but this part of our tour is over and the imagination door has opened once again and our journey continues.

The Ocean

Come with me and we'll conquer the ocean, for the air has changed and become moist and heavy and far overhead we begin to hear a different tune - a musical challenge that belongs to the sea. It sounds like rhythmic pounding, thundering and smashing of wave after wave crashing upon an ocean shore, accented by the high-pitched screeching of gulls.

We have left the woods to follow the slender shadows of the tall sea grasses, pointing the way towards the sounds of the surf. High flying birds swoop in and out of the water, noisily announcing our arrival and shoreline birds strut straight legged, quickly, with match stick legs, on the hardened sand, and then, *it all comes together: the all-encompassing sunlight sweeping under a celestial canopy of blue, streaked with birds diving, cawing, winds stinging and howling, leaving a taste of salt and wetness upon our faces.*

A relentless storm grasps hold of the world
Before us and around us and challenges us
To ride with it and not let go, but -

The Sky

The winds and the waters sense our hesitation to join them, so we accept an alternative: the winds tell us to take one of the golden cords that lie on the sand and tie it around our waist. Once secured, each cord will gently lift us into the air, all the while remaining fastened to the depths of the earth. The cords will not let go of us. We will rise higher and higher until we are floating, gracefully overhead, looking down upon our shadows on the sand below us.

There are some of us who choose to ascend further, until

We have left the blue safety of the heavens behind,
And begin to enter the silent eternal night
that welcomes us on paths of moonbeams and starlight
Exploding into sapphires and emeralds in the sky.
If we glance over our shoulder, we see
where all the glorious sunsets are stored
in case of an evening when the sun is too tired
To ignite the sky and must rely on yesterday's glory,-
Still usable, but never as astounding as the first time.

In order to return to the earth, at any time, we just give a gentle tug on the golden rope and we will float down.

Rainbow Balloons

If a shorter journey is your wish, you may find relaxation and comfort by: lying down comfortably, relaxing slowly, breathing deeply and picturing brightly colored balloons, with long strings, being tied around your waist, your chest, your neck and head, arms and legs. Balloons of every color of the rainbow. Then, with your eyes closed, feel yourself being lifted into the air by the balloons. Try to imagine that you are floating, free of tension, free of pain and filled with calmness. You may come back down at any time, just visualize the air slowly being released from the balloons, or just see yourself slowly and safely, returning to a prone position.

Shortcut

At this time, if you chose, you may program yourself to quickly return to a relaxed state. If you are not in a place where you may fully relax, or lie down, follow the these steps for a "Short Cut to Serenity": first, slowly take in three deep breaths, secondly, choose a pleasant sounding word, (such as aquamarine, rosebud, springtime, love, etc)and repeat it to yourself while lightly pressing both thumbs and forefingers together, focusing on how relaxed all of your muscles feel at this moment.

Tell yourself you will feel this relaxed when you silently repeat your special word and practice this exercise.

End of Tour

We are at the end of our tour. You may return at any time and if you chose, may shorten the tour by taking a less challenging route. You may chose your own place (planet) your own time (the future) or elect to travel solo or not. Three thoughts to keep in mind before and after your excursion

1) How you think is how you feel.
2) To change your feelings, change your thinking.
3) Your body believes every word your mind tells it.

(Shortcut reminder: did you choose your secret word)?

Another journey waits.

There's a Rooster on My Deck

There's a rooster on my deck made of metal. He's painted
Red, green and white. "He's glorious," thought I,
When I saw how his wings were decorated
with red and white stripes. He stood three feet high
On a shelf in a store and to resist him, I could not.
You'd not miss seeing him either, for he stood far above
The rest of the birds, the brightest of the lot.

I took him down from the shelf, gave him to the cashier,
Whilst my husband looked at me as though
I had just stepped in from the stratosphere.
No idea had I, what to say or do with him,
Or where I would put him or where he would be
I just knew my jolly life would turn lonely and grim
If that red metal rooster didn't belong to me.

We decided to perch him on our sturdy deck railing
Where my husband securely strapped him down
So the mightiest of winds would not send him sailing
'Cross the fairways where the golfers are bound.
He strikes a bold posture, gazing out on the fairway
His eyes scanning the golfers as they drive by.
"Maybe I could help them finish their play
And tell them just where their balls do lie."

It appears as though our rooster was cleverly created
To observe the landscape, well-kept and pristine,
For I once heard him comfort a fellow, who unabatedly,
Sobbed, "I could not have hit the ball times thirteen."

Our bird has sense, though his legs and feet are green,
And he'll tell the golf boys of proper decorum and such;
To stay on the cart path and avoid the in between
And by all means, be sure to stay out of the rough.
Lately, I wonder, are we doing something wrong -
To give cheer and good counsel, is it fittin'?
Maybe his opinion just doesn't belong,
We don't want our rooster to be a cheatin'chicken!
Since passing our house and the rooster on the deck
We see the players look happier, without a growl,
They seem so joyful since our rooster, they have met,
We finally decided our fowl is not foul.

So, now, the golfers no longer shout –
"Hey, have you seen my ball?" but ask instead –
What does the rooster say, the one with the clout –
The one with the polka dots on his head?
If we're in a good mood, we'll let the rooster do his thing,
But if not, we'll simply say, "Are you nuts or something?
What do you think we've got on our deck:
A green bellied,
striped red and white wing,
polka dot tail and cockscomb too,
green legged and green footed -

ROOSTER"?
WHO EVER HEARD OF SUCH A THING?

A Valentine

(UPDATED, REVISED, RELOCATED
AND COMPROMISED)

I'm Valentined out, how can there possibly be more to say -
About she loves, he loves, we all love throughout the day
Into the sunrise of the morning, even confessed it at night?
I left love notes on your pillow, even stuffed some out of sight
Into your shoes which made them smaller
which made them much too tight.

Last year I told you that we smooched and hugged and
tickled and grinned,
Rolled our eyes and fussed 'til the cows came in
(they never did)
And screamed and shouted and purred and pouted,
We were ecstatic, romantic, arthritic (now worse, of course) and
dumbfounded.
We held hands while alone at night (did that many times);
Were overwhelmed, understated, misquoted and underrated.
We admired and respected our mutual pluses
And mostly can't remember why all the silly fusses. (Weren't
they silly)?
We minimized, discredited and patted a cheek or two,
Supported (whatever), upheld and bit our tongue until blue.
We tsked, sighed, grumbled and scowled,
We were cute-sie and sweet, flirty and foul.

But last year I didn't remind you, I plumb forgot;
To buy little gifts for me, which would have meant a lot.
Something much more important than a tender gesture or smile,

To Be Brief...

But just a few small trinkets to admire for a while,
Such as: roses, this year, six dozen, I think
Along with candy and yachts and furs (maybe, mink)
With exotic perfumes from the orient and beyond
In satin boxes filled with rubies - of which I'm so fond,
(Silly me).
And - - you know I'm just kidding, what would I do
With all that stuff, when all I ever want is you?
Those boxes of chocolates of which I spoke
Would only broaden my circumference and render you broke.
You're still my Valentine, in the morning or in the night
And you'll know I'm all yours........ if your shoes are too tight.

The Parkinson Rap

So, *this* is my *piece* and I *need* to *say* it;
The *night* before I *meet* my *new* brain *doc*
I get up*tight* and *nervous* and *filled* to the *top* with it -
Anxiety, I *call* it, (in an an*tic*ipatory *way)*-
Anxiety - that *is,* 'cause *I know* what he'll *say:*
"Here, *take* this *pill* and if *that* doesn't *work,*
Then, we'll *stick* you in a *tube" (where* I'm *sure* to *lose* it
Claustro*pho*bia – that *is). So,* I *say:* "please *don't,* I *pray."*
But *why* sup*pose*, for *he* may *not* pro*pose;*
And *just* examine *me* and *state* he's *so* in*clined*
To *treat* me, *treat* me? *Yes,* it's *what* he *said:*
"We can *treat* you" and he *said* it a*gain:* "shall we *treat* you?"

He was *seated* 'cross from *me,* at an *eye* to eye *level*
And with *pupils* so *deep* and *voice* so in*credible*
And *soft* he mostly *whispered,* when he *spoke* his in*tent:*
"What *do* you *think?* Would you *like* to *vent?"*
I said: *"Yes,* but I *thought* that *docs* of the *brain*
Use the *rubber* room and *if* that's in *vain,*
Use a *shiny* metal *beanie* with *cords* at*tached*
But I can *take* it, (if it will *help* my *angst* get a *blast*
Of Elec*tricity*, that is)."
I *pon*dered for a *bit,* then *thought* again,
"Maybe *we* can make a *deal,"* said *I* to my phy*sician*:
"Here are some *alterna*tives that *you* may uti*lize*
To *restore* my *health* and then *you* could pub*licize*
So the *big* guys, like the *AMA* a*ward* you the *big* prize-
(Pulitzer, that *is)."*

To Be Brief...

"My *deal* is:

"You can en*treat* me, be*seech* me, *relieve* me or *bleep* me,
You may *seek* me, de*feat* me, re*store* me, even *adore* me
Or re*treat* with me or *keep* me, re*heat* me, even *greet* me, - - -
But, *please,* please, *please,* just *please* don't *treat* me!"

"You can be *sweet* to me, be*lieve* in me, bom*bard* me or
super*sede* me,
See *through* me, be *mean* to me, *correct* me or even *flatter* me,
You can even *screech* at me, or *keep* me, be dis*crete* with me
(If you *examine* me) –
But, *please,* please, *please,* just *please* don't *treat* me!"

I *think* this new *doc* under*stood* my de*meanor*
He *didn't* have to *say* that *Park*inson's has no re*deemer*,
No *toy,* no *tricks,* no *cure,* or guaran*tee*
But he *doesn't* know I'm a *runner,* a *sprinter*, if *need* be.
And *may*be I can *outrun* that *damned* di*sease*
To the *far* places *of* the mind and *out* of its *reach* –
"Let's *do* it, "said the *doc* and I will *meet* you *there*
As long as *you* accept my *deal,* so *just* to be *fair:*

"You must con*tinue* to *write,* to*day* and every*day.*
You must *challenge* your *brain* to *work* in every *way;*
To *stir* up the *neurons* and *dopa*mine *too,*
Til you *finally realize* that *all* you can *do*
Is to *catch* a fast *horse* and *jump* on its *back*
And *ride* it to a *frenzy* and *never* look *back."*
So the *doc* said his *piece* and *I* did *too.*
There's *nothing* more to *say,* to *me* or to *you.*

Guess I'll *walk* in the *country*

And *play* in a *pile* of hay

And *maybe* all *this*

Will *go* aw*ay*

Far *away*

My Son Took Me Sailing on Sunday Afternoon

My son took me sailing on a Sunday afternoon
And I thought I'd see the sun glistening on calm waters,
Shining down upon the deck; serene and wistful, with
A timid breeze cooling me from the shore, instead:

I saw vessels with towering masts charging the skies
And yearning for the stars. I heard mariners' lusty sea shanties
Echoing from watery tombs along forgotten trade routes once laden
With spices, silks and exotic perfumes. I could hear their deep voices
Wailing gruff and low, weaving in and out from the cold
remains below.
I watched white sails of regal majesty slapping hard into the winds:
"*Look Up! Come About! "Jibe Ho!*" comes the command from
The captain who stood fast at the wheel, as he took his stand -
My son, that commander, who took me sailing on a Sunday afternoon

My son took me sailing on a Sunday afternoon
And we drifted along as one is bound to do
Without winds to take us to a port of call,
Hence, ended our sail and that night, I dreamt, instead:

The commander released his power and challenged the winds to
Hold back the raging surge of waves frothing at the height of
their crest
Until later, as the wind began to lull, he tamed his vessel and
Lowered the sails, then rested awhile on still waters of the night,
Watching stars as they trembled against a silent black sky:

Guiding his way, his solace, his light; that commander,
My son, who took me sailing on a Sunday afternoon.

My son took me sailing on a Sunday afternoon
Coaxing his ship to heel and to give up her wayward
Bend and yield to his persuasion, 'til finally
Wearied and like a woman, stretching out as in a dream,
The ship becomes calmed and supple, yielding to his command
Still sounding in my head: *'Look Up! Come About! Jibe Ho!"*
Said the commander, my son, who took me sailing on that
Sunday afternoon.

Speak it Out!

Oh, speak it out, I say. If you have something that needs to be said,
Don't speak above it, around it or under the bed,
Just speak it out and see where it goes.
It probably won't hurt you or kill you
Though you never really know.
Maybe it will.

You say you get tongue tied, though
I've never seen one so disposed.
So just loosen the knot
Or tell her you forgot,
Which won't buy you any accolades
Or even a glass of lemonade.

Just speak it aloud even if the famous
Bard and poet may never suspect
You speak the same brogue that he's heard ever since
A Juliet first lamented of a new love possessed:
"What if Romeo doth fear to speak out my name
And cries out for "Eunice" instead?"

She'll never know how much you love her
If you don't tell her so.
She'll never suspect your longing, if you're too shy to let it go.
If you don't ask her to be your bonnie bride
She'll never say yes or for that matter – no,
Which is maybe just as well, 'cause you can always ask her
next year, if she hasn't said yes – or married Joe.

A Visit from Julenissen

"I had a mule; her name was Sal – fifteen years on the Erie Canal. She's a good ole worker and a good ole pal, fifteen years on the Erie Canal." That's how the song goes, except our canal was named The Barge Canal. It really did have barges, gigantic barges, but they weren't pulled by mules. The house I lived in with my parents and two sisters was on top of a hill that overlooked the canal. Sometimes when a barge was approaching, it would sound its horn and my sisters and I would run to the edge of the hill and wave at the passing barge. Then it would sound the horn again. I pretended our house on the hill was my castle, and I remember living there from ever since I can remember. It was like a fairy tale to me, because whenever I walked outside of my house in the morning it was as beautiful as it was in the fairy tales: the glorious sun would say hello to me and songbirds of every kind and size and color, sang their songs to me and the wind fluffed my hair and beckoned me to dance down to the little pollywog pools, where I looked for toads and then searched in the wild strawberry fields for their sweet warm treasures. (I would have said their "bright red berries," but fairy tale talk is different.)

My name is Ingrid and I live with my mother, father, and two older sisters; one sister is eight years older than I am and the other is four years older. My parents and oldest sister were born in Copenhagen, Denmark and my other sister and I were born in the states. We all understand Danish (and English) and in our house we speak both languages.

Most days, as far as I can tell, my two sisters would leave for school and my father said he was "going to work." I guess I was too young for school, so I would be home all day long, playing by myself and sometimes, I would get lonely and would wish it was time for my sisters to come home.

Then there were days when my mother and I would visit some of her friends and they might pick us up in their car or when we could, we would walk. I had just passed by the strawberry patch and had started to look for dandelions and daisies when I heard my mother calling my name, "Come on, Ingrid, we're going to walk to Mrs. Andersen's house." Though it was a long walk, it was fun for the two of us to walk into the country.

Shortly after we arrived, Mrs. Andersen went to the attic and brought down the most beautiful doll in the whole world, at least *my* world and asked me if I wanted to follow her to a nearby room and play with the beautiful creature. Of course, I said I would. The doll was big with thick curly golden hair and was dressed in finer clothes than I had ever seen. She wore a red velveteen jacket and skirt, trimmed with fur and on her feet were perfect, untarnished shoes with a matching handbag. She was elegant and fine and when she was handed to me, I couldn't remember all of the dos and don'ts, but that didn't matter. I could tell, by just looking at her, that this doll would not tolerate or allow any rough handling. As I laid her down, her blue glass eyes with heavy eyelashes, flicked closed and she whimpered: "Ma-a-a---Ma-a-a-a-.

I pretended she could really speak and played with her for

awhile, talking for the two of us, but even though she was so elegant, I still felt lonely whenever it was her turn to talk, and she couldn't, of course. I remember thinking, as we were getting ready to leave, "I wish I had a doll who could really talk and play with me and then I wouldn't be so lonely."

Another home we used to visit was where Aunt Sue lived. Since all my relatives are in Denmark, she wasn't really an aunt, we just called her that. Aunt Sue didn't have any dolls to play with, but she had boxes and boxes of buttons; all different sizes, colors, shapes, some with sparkling stones, other with funny stripes and she would ask me to sort them into different piles. I don't know why, but it seemed awfully important to her. Sometimes I would talk to the buttons and ask them why they were not being used on some clothes and why they had to be sorted. But again, it was just me who answered and not the buttons.

One of my favorite places to visit was the home of Mrs. and Mrs. Christiansen. He was a carpenter, and it was at his house I first saw wooden furniture for dolls made by Mr. Christiansen. He would bring out his wonders such as: a doll's high chair, a crib and best of all, a doll's cradle, made of gleaming dark brown wood, on rockers that softly caused the bed to sway and tilt back and forth, rocking the doll to sleep. I always hoped, every time that I visited him, that maybe this time he would say, "Ingrid, would you like to take this cradle home for your dolls?" He never did ask, but I would make believe he did.

I didn't have very many dolls of my own, but I think my favorite was my Sonja Henie doll. Sonja Henie was a famous

Olympic star figure skater and the dolls looked just like her. My sister and I both received such a doll last Christmas and we played with our dolls almost every day, except, lately, when the dolls would be missing. We wouldn't be able to find them and just when we were about to ask our mother if she knew where they might be, they would appear again. On this Christmas Eve, we discovered what had been happening. We opened our gifts and inside a box were our Sonja Henie dolls, beautifully dressed in knit outfits of jackets, skirts, hats, gloves, dresses, everything you could imagine, including new ice skating outfits. Our mother had to borrow the dolls, temporarily, to make sure the new clothes that she had been making, fit properly.

As I dressed my doll in all of her lovely outfits, I wished she would be able to ice skate for me, and I would pretend that she could, but I really knew better.

Whenever I played with Mrs. Andersen's beautiful big doll, or aunt Sue's buttons, or saw Mr. Christiansen's cradle or whenever I played with my Sonja Henie doll, I would go to bed that night and wish and wish real hard that they could play with me – really – like talking and moving and just playing games and having fun and then, maybe, if they could, I wouldn't feel so lonely anymore, so much of the time. Then one night I remembered, after I had gone to bed, some stories our daddy had read to us about magic elves and the miracles they could do, and I decided as I closed my eyes that I would ask him all about the elves in the morning.

After I woke up and thought about what I had planned to do, I discovered it was not so easy. I didn't want my dad to worry about me or think I was an unhappy person. But then I thought about it and decided I could tell him about my feelings in a way that he might know of some of the little elves that he talked about who might help me out. I asked if there were perhaps some extra elves who had nothing to do, who could turn all the toys into real live people and he explained that he would call upon the Danish Santa Claus or Julenissen, (Santa's name in Danish) and if I were a really good girl, then Santa would visit me and I could ask him about my request.

"But when will the Julenissen come and how will I know him?" I asked.

"When you go to bed tonight and close your eyes and whisper his name, he will visit you," my father explained. "He is a wonderfully kind person and has been a personal friend of mine. He is sure to help you."

I gave my daddy a big hug and told him I would probably go to bed early tonight so I could whisper Santa's ("whoops, Julenissen's") name.

That night I lay in my bed and watched the shadows of the trees outside my window dance on my bedroom wall and the snowflakes trickle down the window pane and I whispered, "Julenissen, please visit me, just for a little while, please visit me."...then, in the soft quiet of the night I heard little bells tinkle and the still air seemed to have the scent of Christmas: of warm cookies baking and peppermint sticks and a pine log flickering in the fireplace and I heard a small voice say, "Hello, sweet Ingrid. I heard you calling me and I think I know why. You see, I keep very close track of good children like you and your dear father would like to see you happier and I told him, when he called me earlier, I would help you. All you need to do is to listen carefully and do as I say. Are you willing to do that?" he queried.

"Oh, yes, Julenissen, oh yes. I promise I will faithfully do whatever you ask of me."

With that, the friendly little gentleman sat on the edge of my bed and explained, "I will help you by giving you the eternal gift of imagination. It is a gift that has been with man ever since man was born; some have received it, many would like to achieve it, many have abused it by ignoring it and many have had the angels of the skies leave it at their doorstep. It is given to you because we know you are good and you will use it to enhance the world around you and cause others to fill their hearts with blithe spirits so pure and true. As you will believe in sweet tempered dolls and toys through the use of your imagination, you will soon discover ways to gladden the lives of others, either through kind words, the written word, through music or song or in ways you have yet to discover. You will be able to use it right away and it will grow and grow and be with you for the rest of your life. As you use it you will learn more and more about it, but for now, you will feel less lonely and it will give you the happiness you seek."

Ingrid was pleased, excited and confused. She asked, "But how will I know how to use it?"

"It will be very simple," answered Jule Nissen. "When you want something to happen, like a doll talking to you, close your eyes, for just a little bit, and tell yourself, "I can see and hear the doll talking and walking and playing and it will happen. If you do that enough times, after a while, you won't even have to say the words, it will just happen when you think the words. And if you think the words enough, you will develop a feeling of love and happiness towards others. Some people say that's magic, but it isn't. It is just the way the world was meant to be."

"If I get mixed up sometimes and not sure how to use my new gift, may I whisper for you again, Julenissen?"

"Of course, Ingrid, and if I'm awfully busy sometime, ask your father to help you, for I have explained all of this to him."

Ingrid was so excited about her special gift that she couldn't wait to tell her father. "Daddy, wait til you hear what the Julenissen said to me and how I'm going to use it, and….and….

"Yes, yes, Ingrid, I know, for the Julenissen wanted me to know so I could help you if you needed it. Let's just keep it between the two of us for now and see what happens, shall we?" Ingrid agreed

Dolls, Buttons, a Cradle and a Mouse

And so it happened, that it was just a few days later following Julenissen's visit, when Ingrid and her mother were walking to Mrs. Andersen's house and this time it was her mother who could barely keep up with Ingrid's pace. "Oh, please, mother, let's hurry and get there," said Ingrid, pulling on her mother's arm." I really want to play with that beautiful big doll." Soon, they approached the front door and there was Mrs. Andersen welcoming them and offering coffee, hot chocolate and pastries. After Ingrid had politely sipped her drink, she could contain herself no longer and said, "Mrs. Andersen, do you suppose I could play with your big doll and if it's alright with you, I don't mind playing with her in the attic. There's plenty of room up there and I won't bother you and my mother with my singing and make believe playing."

Mrs. Andersen was pleased to escort Ingrid to the attic, turned on plenty of lights and showed her to a comfortable sofa and chairs upon which to enjoy her playing. After Ingrid thanked her and waited for her to leave, she breathed a sigh of relief for she was so excited to begin the first use, that she knew of, of her new imagination.

Ingrid sat the doll beside her on the sofa. She closed her eyes, briefly, and said to herself: "I can hear this doll talking to me, I can see this doll walking and moving about, I can…"

"Good morning, Ingrid," said a small happy voice. "I am so

happy you came back to visit me. I would love to play some games with you and dance with you, see?....like this…."and the beautiful doll gently took Ingrids' hands and the two of them danced on their tip toes across the floor. The doll started to sing as they danced: "My name is Belinda

So happy am I
For a have a new friend
Who is lovelier than I"

Ingrid, barely catching her breath after her dance with the real live doll, and after getting over her surprise and shock, kindly corrected the doll, "Oh, no. No one could ever be lovelier than you and you can talk, and walk and dance and you made all my dreams come true."

"Not so, not me, I didn't do it, you did," the doll responded. "Your imagination made your dreams come true and we shall play together whenever we chose."

"Belinda, this is all so wonderful, but what will happen to us after I leave here today" I probably shouldn't ask too many questions, but how will we see each other again," questioned Ingrid.

"This is only the first time you have used your new gift," Belinda replied. Next time you will remember and just do what Julenissen suggested. Whenever you want us to meet and play just close your eyes and we will be together, talking, walking, dancing...always...you'll see.

Ingrid went home that night and was so thrilled with her

adventure with the doll named Belinda, she could barely sleep, but within the next few weeks she continued to use her imagination, having ever so many joyous times with her new playmate.

The next few times she practiced using her new gift were when she and her mother visited the carpenter, Mr. Christiansen, and there, once again, he brought out the polished, gleaming, wooden cradle that Ingrid so loved to look at and pretend she would put her doll into the soft bed. However, this time, things did not happen as before. This time when the cradle was brought out, Ingrid briefly closed her eyes and imagined her doll lying in the precious cradle and Mr. Christensen said, "Ingrid, do you think your doll could use a new bed and would be happy to sleep in this cradle?"

Ingrid was stunned and confused, because she didn't want to do anything to take away the joy that the elderly carpenter experienced with his cradle. She started to say, "Oh no, I couldn't take this beautiful bed, it's yours…." "Nonsense, my dear, what is an old man like me going to do with this doll's cradle? If I thought for a minute you wouldn't treat it well, well, that's a different story. But it's time to pass it on and I can't think of anyone I'd rather give it to than you."

Ingrid was so happy with her new cradle, that she shared it with her friends who now came to her house to visit and play with their dolls, the cradle and Ingrid.

Ingrid was delighted with her new friends, and one day, when they were playing, she almost told them about her experience with Aunt Sue and the buttons. She nearly said that when she and her mother last visited Aunt Sue and Aunt Sue brought out the buttons, Ingrid had quite a different game with them. When she first looked at the buttons, she closed her eyes briefly and imagined the buttons whispering, singing, talking to each other and to her, then opened her eyes – and they did – they actually did. She never laughed and giggled so much in her whole life. (The buttons made up rhymes like):

"One two button your shoe, button your hat
and button your blouse,
Three four we need one more
button, 'cause one just rolled away
With a mouse!!!"

After all, it was not very often that one could have long talks, games, riddles and jokes with a bushel of buttons. Ingrid thought it was so funny, she almost laughed aloud on the way home.

Ingrid had saved her Sonja Henie doll until last for trying out her new gift of imagination.

Finally, one afternoon, when her mother was busy starting the preparations for dinner, Ingrid took her figure skating doll into her room, briefly closed her eyes, wished the doll would talk, dance and most of all, figure skate. She squeezed her eyes shut and waited for sounds of the doll coming to life. She was so anxious about her gift not working. But it did work. She opened her eyes just a little and there, before her, was an ice-skating rink and her talented doll spinning around in circles, smiling and waving at Ingrid. "Hello, Ingrid," the doll shouted. "If you like, you can pretend that you're my size and come onto the rink and skate with me."

"Hello, Sonja doll. You skate just wonderfully. I'm so glad you can be a part of my world. I've hoped and wished so hard, for so long, and now you're here. Thank you, thank you, so much."

With that, the doll skated to the edge of the rink, extended her hand to Ingrid and as Ingrid took her hand, she immediately became the doll's size, stepping onto the ice and as if she had skated all her life, and glided away with the doll. Ingrid and the doll were such a happy sight.

As they skated 'cross the ice, Ingrid told Sonja all about the new cradle that she could sleep in tonight. Sonja replied with joy what a wonderful treat that will be as long as she doesn't have to share it with a button and a mouse! You could hear Ingrid and Sonja laugh all the way across the ice skating rink.

Puppy Love and Chicken Pox

I was standing on our hill, waving to a barge sail by, when my sisters ran to get me, and breathlessly told me about some young men who had just arrived at our house. We went back to the house and sat in the living room with our parents and listened to their story.

They had recently arrived in the States from the Danish Naval Training ship, and decided to stay in America and were looking for jobs and places to live.

My daddy was President of the Danish Brotherhood and our home was always open to Danish people and regular people, too. Of course, my father welcomed the young men and they moved in with us until they could get settled and live on their own.

There were three fellows who stayed at our house and others who frequently came to visit and to dinner. We all enjoyed their company, especially me. Maybe I was a little spoiled and being the baby of the family. I guess I got a lot of attention.

Two and sometimes three of the young men would take me on a short walk to a nearby candy store and when we arrived they told me to pick out whatever candy I wanted. They even gave me a little bag and told me to fill it to the top. No one had ever done that for me before!

They would also spend time playing with me and telling me stories. Sometimes, when my parents weren't looking, they would make funny faces and we would laugh so and when my parents turned around, the young men would just pretend they had never done anything.

There was one young man whom I particularly liked. His name was Earling Sundeau. He was so pretty to look at; he had black, thick, wavy hair and beautiful blue eyes and would always sit with me and talk with me and I thought he was just wonderful. I heard someone once talk about a "puppy dog crush" and I'm not real sure what it means, but I had an idea it had something to do with the nice feelings I had for Earling.

One summer day, our whole family went for a drive and Earling joined us. It turned out to be a long drive and on the way home, I fell asleep. Earling picked me up and put me on his lap so I could be more comfortable. As our car arrived home, I woke up, but pretended to be asleep, hoping that Earling would carry me into the house which he did, all the way up the stairs and to my bed. He laid me down, and left the room so my older sisters could come in and undress me and put me to bed. As soon as they started to undress me, I opened my eyes and laughed. I must have really surprised them at my pretending to be asleep, because they really laughed, and all three of us just giggled and laughed and laughed.

Other summer or fall days, Earling would sing songs to me, tell stories and take me for walks,

I didn't know enough to say he was gentle and kind, I just knew I loved being with him.

Then, I got sick. I think my mother said I had something that chickens get and some days I was put into my parents' bedroom with the shades drawn and the curtains closed, making the room dark and gloomy. I was alone, sitting up in their big bed and had it not been for my talking doll, I don't know what I would have done. Once in a while my sisters would come in to see, me and my daddy always did because he was so wonderful. One afternoon, there was a knock on the door, and after I said, "Come in" the door opened and in walked a lady, whom I knew as Alice, about the same age as Earling and behind her walked Earling. (Earling was about 19 or 20, and I was five.) They were both very nice to me, gave me some presents (probably something like a coloring book and crayons) and that was also very nice and they were very, very nice to each other. I hated her. I didn't know why I hated her, I only knew that I wanted her off the face of the earth as soon as possible. Earling came over to my bedside, held my hand, gave me a kiss on the cheek and then they both left. After they left I had a funny feeling in my chest and my stomach, and tears started to fall. It made me feel like I had felt before when I wanted something really bad and I couldn't have it.

After a while, the feeling went away and I almost didn't even remember it, but I do remember thinking if that was "Puppy love," I sure didn't want it to come back, not now, or ever; same with chicken pox.

Later, when I was better, Alice and Earling came to our house and I went for a walk with them, between them and holding their hands. That felt good and we were all very nice.

Her Royal Highness

It was only weeks away from Christmas and my mother and I were making plans for the big holiday.

"Well, Ingrid," my mother said; "are you going to help me get ready for Julenissen?" (That was Danish for Santa Claus)

"Of course, I am and are we going to have marzipan and Christmas cookies?"

"Oh, yes, lots of marzipan!" she replied.

"But Mother, (I always called her Mother), why is it that some of the kids in school say that we don't celebrate Christmas the way we should? They say we should celebrate on December 25th and not on December 24."

"You just tell them that the Danish Santa Claus gets up earlier in Denmark so he can leave there on time to get to America before the little American children wake up."

"I like that he gets up earlier and I love having Christmas dinner and presents on the 24th because then I can stay up late and play with my presents and not have to wait until morning."

"I like it too, Ingrid, but now it's time to meet your father at the turn of the sidewalk. He'll be there almost any minute!"

My father walked to and from work and each day when he was walking home, at a special bend in the sidewalk, a little ways from our house, I would run out and wait for him. I could see him coming in the distance, getting closer and closer, bigger and bigger, until finally, I couldn't wait another second, I would burst forward, run as fast as I could and jump into his waiting arms. He was so big and tall and strong. He would lift me up and carry me for awhile as I gave him the biggest hug that I possibly could and we usually ended the walk home with me holding his hand and skipping along side of him, as we both sang:

"Skippity Hop, To the barber shop
To buy a piece of Candy
One for you and one for me
And one for sister Annie."

As we entered the house, my mother called out, "Come into the living room, everyone. Your daddy's home and I have a special surprise for you." We all hugged daddy and sat down and waited for the special surprise."

Our mother explained, "We received this big box from the mailman today, and I can see it's from Denmark. I didn't open it for I thought we might all want to do that together." The box was huge and since Christmas was just around the corner, I guessed it must be presents.

After we tore open the lids, my mother carefully lifted out the most beautiful navy blue taffeta sailor dresses, with big square collars, with white cord piping, one for each of us girls.

My mother read the letter that came with the dresses and told us they were handmade by our grandmother, our father's mother ("fa-mor" in Danish) and sent to us with love as our Christmas present.

My oldest sister, Karen, excitedly said, "Oh, I can't wait until we can wear them? Will it be soon?"

My mother was about to answer, when my father commented instead, "It looks as though there's more than one person here today with a surprise. I have some very important and exciting news for all of us."

We jumped up and down asking for his news and after quieting down, our father told us, "I received a phone call today from the Danish Embassy in New York City, looking to speak with the President of our local Chapter of The Danish Brotherhood and as you know, since that's me, I spoke with him."

At this very point, we had all hushed and were very quietly listening to each important word.

Daddy continued, "The news is that the Crown Princess Ingrid is touring the United States and will be taking a train through this part of the country as part of her tour. If we can have a welcoming party or a small reception ready for her, she will schedule the train to make a stop at the train station in our city."

We were all so thrilled, and our father said the major problem was that it all had to happen within the next few days.

I could tell my daddy was very busy working on whatever had to be done to make this big event happen and had received bad news that our mayor and other important people, who would have welcomed the Crown Princess, would be out of town.

I do not know how it all came about, but my father was able to take care of everything. He arranged a welcoming party, notified the newspapers, who said they would send reporters, and had a small band ready. He then asked my mother to make a small bouquet of flowers from her garden, and to dress me in my white coat and white French beret and then asked me, "Ingrid, would you be willing to welcome the Crown Princess and give these pretty flowers to her?"

I thought that all of this news was thrilling and exciting and told my daddy that I would love to.

The big day found all of us gathered on the platform of the train station, awaiting the arrival, when someone shouted, "Here it comes!"

We were all cheering and waving when the train finally came to a stop. I was next to my daddy in the front line of all the people who started to push their way closer and of course, I was so little that pretty soon I couldn't even see the train. When my father lifted me up with my flowers in one hand, and someone pushed a pretty Danish flag in my other hand, which I waved and waved and then....saw the princess in the window of the train and she smiled and waved back at me! Suddenly, she disappeared. I was about to ask my father what to do, when the door to the last car of the train opened and out she walked, smiling, looking, and then walked right over to me. She was beautiful! She leaned over to get closer to me and I handed her the flowers. She said, "Oh, they're lovely, thank you."

Then, she looked at the Danish flag and asked, "Is this for me, too?"

Somewhat unsure of my answer, I said, "No, it belongs to my mother."

She then shook my hand and said, "It was wonderful to meet you."

Then it happened so quickly, she turned and was gone, inside of her private coach, smiling and waving goodbye to me through her window.

I was so thrilled I could hardly think of anything else for days, and even as I grew older, whenever I thought of that experience in my life, it still brought a warm, quiet excitement to my heart.

With so much excitement in our house, we almost forgot about our new sailor dresses and the Danish Christmas party. It would be our opportunity to wear them and to dance and sing and eat all the wonderful food that everyone brought. Part of the evening, my father would play the Danish folk dances and songs on the piano along with two other fellows who played their violins. During some of the dances, we would all stand in a huge circle, hold hands and dance and sing until we couldn't dance or sing anymore. It was a wonderful party, especially with our new dresses and our hair curled by mother's hot curling iron.

At the close of the evening, the children would line up to say hello to a Julenissen (Santa Claus) and receive what we thought was the most wonderful gift: each of us was given a large orange and a small box of about ten candies. On the way home in the car, I sat in the back seat with my presents on my lap, holding them, treasuring them, but most of all, I was treasuring the feeling of happiness that I received from the people who sang and danced and feasted with us. Other Danes, and regular people too.

A Bouquet of Lilacs

Have you ever felt you have known a flower for all of your life? No, I don't mean you were introduced to the flower, as if to make its acquaintance, but that somehow you always knew about it - its shape, its scent, its very presence and its being. That may sound silly, but I know that I have. I have known lilacs since I can remember myself. I first knew them when I was very little, before school, even. I used to play with my dolls underneath a tall huge lilac tree. I was able to make a little house for myself under its branches that unfurled overhead into thick lavender blossoms reaching towards more purple blossoms and I would look up through their flowers and see the blue sky overhead, far away and very high up. The flowers smelled sweeter and nicer than roses. In fact, they smelled the best of any flower I knew. I felt safe in that place; it was secret, it was quiet, it was mine. My dolls also loved it. I think it was because of that place, that later on, as I grew, I always fell in love with every lilac I saw.

Well, you can imagine my delight when my parents said "let's go to Highland Park and look at the lilacs! In fact, girls, come here for a moment and I will read a paragraph from the newspaper to you, about the lilacs, " beckoned my father. "In 1892, colonists carried slips of 20 varieties of lilacs from England to Rochester, New York where they started a municipal park culminating in 500 varieties covering 22 acres of the 155 acre park. The exhibition of lilacs is the largest in North America. Currently, hundreds of thousands of visitors from around the world have traveled to view the blooms and today, if you like, we can be a part of those many peoples."

We were overjoyed and ready to go. Highland Park! Even the name sounded like a heavenly place, high up over the land in the clouds. No cars were allowed in the park, only people walking. I imagine that at one time, it was a forest of nothing but trees, shrubs and bushes, until the folks from England brought the flower to us. There were walking paths everywhere with benches along the way, as I suppose people would get tired of walking and looking at so many flowers.

The lilacs wore every breath-taking imaginable shade of purple, such as: midnight purple, plush purple, light lavender purple, even pink and almost white purple to pure white. People could walk at their leisure and sit at their leisure and just look and breathe in the perfume the lilacs were kind enough to share with us. I looked at the lilacs differently than others. First of all, I had to because I walked slower than the others,(namely, the adults), and because I was smaller. If you're smaller, it takes you longer. But I looked at the lilacs differently because I looked at them *harder,* because if I did I thought I would remember them longer when I went to bed at night and I thought I might see them in my dreams.

But wait, I haven't told you the whole story. Underneath every lilac tree and tall bush, (well, *almost* every tree and bush), there were pansies; thousands of pansies. It's true and in colors of purple, white, yellow orange, pink, even blue. I couldn't count all the colors, and do you know what they were doing? They were smiling at me. Yes, really, pansies can smile. Well, I suppose they smiled at others too and I couldn't help but to smile right back at all the pansies. I felt a little sorry for the grown-ups because they were so big and tall they couldn't see the pansies as close up as I could, but my parents would stop to look at them and I think they smiled back too. My parents and some of the older people would slow down to give us smaller people enough time to look some more so we could remember all of the magnificent colors and fragrances that surrounded us during our tour.

On the way home, I made up a song about the flowers and my adventure:

"Lilacs come in lavender and are so tall I wonder
Do they see the pansies sweet, that blossom at their feet?"

That night I did not mind going to bed because I was pretty tired from all the walking we did in the park. I wondered if when I closed my eyes and let my imagination take over, would I see the park any differently than when I was there earlier today? My imagination has always been a good thing and has been wonderful to have, so, I let myself lay down upon my bed, after saying goodnight and saying my prayers, and pretend I was in the park again.......

....and it happened, only this time, I was alone in the park and the sun was going down. The sky was pink and orange and light purple and reflected its colors on the purple flowers. It was quiet and the scent of the flowers mingled with the breezes wandering by. I walked along a wide path, with clusters of lilacs draped on both sides of me, when, directly ahead of me, there appeared a beautiful lady, dressed in pale wisps of flowing, lavender gown, with long golden tresses, braided and intertwined with lilacs, encircling her head and falling gently down her shoulders and smiling and gently approaching me, greeting me softly, saying, "Hello, Ingrid, I am known as the lady of the lilacs. Do you mind if I talk to you?" I was so startled I couldn't speak, so she continued, "The lilacs have chosen me to speak for them. This is a special night for them and it is celebrated only once a year. It is called 'The Night of the Starsinging Lights.' Together, you and I, tonight, will light up all the blossoms of every lilac in the park. I have a lilac branch for you and one for me and we can glide through the entire park and wherever you touch your lilac branch to another branch, it will light up with all shades of purple, just like the lilacs all around us.

I finally found I was able to speak and asked, "How will I reach the ones way up high, will you help me light those?"

"Of course, I will. But for now, just take my hand and glide among the lilacs. They're waiting for us to start."

We began to touch the flowers and as we did, the blooms began to sing haunting soft melodies, as if coming from a hidden place but not quite sure where. The melodies grew and grew, and as the lights became many, so did the songs increase their heavenly sounds. "Where is the music coming from?" I asked the lady.

"It's coming from deep within the blooms who have been waiting to sing and play their music for a pure little girl with a gift of imagination, for the music will be heard only by her. It appears that you are the gifted one and only you and I can hear the music," replied the lady of the lilacs."

"I never knew that music could be so strange, almost like from another world, but then still close by. I'll remember it always."

"Come now, Ingrid, I must get you back to your bed. First,

allow me to lift you up and carry you and we'll float upwards a little and now, look up, look down and all around you." And I did and never saw such a magnificent sight with the black sky filled with starlights above us, yet mingling with the lilacs now full with sparkling lights and music playing everywhere, above and below us.

"How did all this happen? Has it always been like this? Can everyone see it and hear it?" Ingrid asked, impatiently and full of curiosity and questions.

The lady of the lilacs replied, "No, Ingrid, only people who have opened their mind and their spirit to let the wonders of the universe enter; only those who will share their imagination, as you do and give it away to fill the hearts of others, only those will experience the essence of connecting with all life forms, and as the joy is shared it becomes an unending circle of being, of light and life."

"It's so glorious, will I be able to come back and see it again?" I inquired.

"Ah, Ingrid, you know how to do that. Just briefly close your eyes and imagine., but now, take my hand and I'll guide you home." I took the beautiful lady's hand and felt as though I was beginning to float and next thing I knew, I was in my bed, in my room in my house, slowly opening my eyes.

"Was I really in a park with a lady? Did I ever really leave my bed? Was it a dream or my imagination?"

"Wherever it was, I saw it, I felt it, I was there and it will fill my heart with joy forever, I know it will, I just know it will."

Paper Dolls

"I'm going to buy a paper doll that I can call my own, a doll that other fellas cannot steal," are words taken from a song called "Paper Dolls." One that I knew during a time when I loved playing with them and it was also during a time when people were killing one another, a time called World War II. It was very confusing to me. I truly did not know why so many soldiers were being killed and why it was happening. Our teachers tried to explain the reasons, but it was very hard to understand. One day people would be crying in the streets and later would be singing silly, as well as sad songs and doing a dance called the "Jitterbug." I guess you could call it a time of contrasts. Everyday life seemed inside out and sometimes upside down. Some of the songs were: "Bye Bye Baby," "Shoo Shoo Baby," "There'll be Bluebirds Over the White Cliffs of Dover" and "When the Lights Go On Again, All Over the World" and songs about soldiers going to war to fight for our country. The songs were written and played in order to boost our morale and keep our spirits up for the soldiers who were fighting and for the folks at home.

On the home front, there were many changes we had to learn and new laws we had to obey. We had to practice drills called "air raids" which were a set of rules of what to do should enemy planes attack us. The air raid started with the sound of a loud siren indicating that all lights were to be turned off and black drapes that we had hung around each window, had to be tightly closed. After several minutes of screaming sirens, wailing throughout the entire city, they finally stopped and we sat in hushed silence, listening and hoping we would not hear any enemy bombers overhead. Every now and then we heard an air raid warden, who patrolled the darkened streets, warn someone about a light that hadn't been turned off, or tell someone else to take cover. I was scared. We were all scared. We could also relate to what other countries were going through by attending movies, especially those depicting the horror of the bombing of England. Those movies were terrifying.

Finally, after we heard the long single note siren, the sound of the "all clear," we took in a deep breath of relief.

It was during this frightening time that I had started to collect paper dolls which meant cutting out some cardboard figures along with many outfits of paper clothes, each doll having its own set of appropriate outfits. I would dress the dolls, pretend through my imagination, they were real and I'd talk with them and, of course, they would talk with me. I knew it wasn't real, but I loved pretending. Besides, if I talked with them and pretended they were real, then why couldn't I pretend the war wasn't real and pretend it wasn't there?

It became harder and harder to pretend the war wasn't real. Lately, I've been taking my paper dolls into my bedroom to play with, because my parents wanted to hear the latest news of the war from the radio in our living room:....."Thousands of soldiers killed in France today and thousands more in Normandy....... leaving the coastline waters running red with their blood. The outlook looks grim, very bad for the allies......"

"So, paper dolls," I would say, (and sometimes out loud, so I couldn't hear the awful news from the radio), "what would you like to do today? Shall I dress you and your family in shorts and we'll all go on a (make-believe) picnic?"

"Girls," my mother instructed, "here are your weekly monies to take to school to buy stamps for your coupon books that need to be filled so you can give it to the government to buy war bonds that will buy tanks and bombs.

"OK, mom."

"A picnic," I said to my paper dolls, Yes! "What shall we take with us to eat? Hot dogs and buns? and let's take our swimming suits and……"

At our dinner table that night our dad told us we had to cut back on buying sugar, butter and meats and we had to save our left over grease in tin cans and take it to stores who would send it on to help build guns and machines. He also told us that ladies could no longer buy silk stockings because the silk would be used to make parachutes.

After dinner I went to my bedroom and there were my paper dolls, waiting for me, just for me, and we played games and talked.

Later, that night, after everyone had gone to bed, I heard my parents quietly talking: "If the Nazis' come into our house, if they open our front door and barge right on in," my mother was whispering, "I think we should do away with ourselves and not let them take us prisoners…."

"Sh-h-h-h-," my father interrupted, "don't talk like that. That's not going to happen and we don't want to scare the girls. Let's not talk like that again."

I took some of my paper dolls to bed with me that night and hugged them real close to me. Just in case they felt scared and they felt like crying, I made up a song and sang it to them:

"Hush, little children, watch the full moon
As it throws light on the marsh and around the lagoon
It will gather all the stars that brighten the dark sky
And they will enfold you and hold you til the sunrise is nigh.
So, sing a lullaby and sleep, sing a lullaby and dream
And morning will bring candy cane rainbows and
lollipop sunbeams

As the war continued and men kept leaving to fight battles and kept dying, and not returning, there were more and more changes as all families tried to do whatever they could, to help our national effort.

One morning, our parents told us that our mother would no longer be at home during lunch time and that we would have to make our own lunch. Our mother had decided to work in a factory making airplanes and as many women were doing, for the first time in their lives, joined the work force. We said we were able to take care of our lunches, it's just that changes were unsettling and we wondered when things were ever going to be normal again.

By now, I had a wonderful collection of paper dolls. I kept each set that included the dolls and their clothes, in their own separate container; boxes that used to contain gloves and were a perfect place for the dolls. I kept the boxes in a special drawer located under our bay window seat; a drawer that had been set aside just for my private use. I was very proud of my paper dolls and had become very attached to them, that's why, when one day when I came home from school and as always went directly to my drawer to pick out the set with which I would play, I couldn't believe my eyes when I opened the drawer and it was empty! It was empty of every box of paper dolls I had ever owned!

"Mother! What happened? What happened to all of my paper dolls?" I ran to her side, tears running down my cheeks. "Do you know where they are?"

"Of course," she said, as she patted my head. "I needed to clean out those drawers today and put the boxes into a large paper sack in the kitchen."

I ran to the kitchen and saw there was no sack. "But, where is it?" I implored.

"Your father must have put it out of the way, he'll tell us when he gets home."

Later, we all discovered that my father thought it was trash to be tossed out and he put it out with other bags for the pickup that had already taken place.

I didn't mean to make anyone feel badly, but I couldn't help the tears; they just kept coming. My make-believe friends were gone, never to return. When they were with me, they helped to make the mixed up days feel like they were before the killing started; normal, safe and full of birds singing – not sirens wailing.

The next day I was asked by my parents to join them and my sisters in our living room, Everyone was sitting down and smiling funny, little, half smiles. I couldn't help but wonder what it was all about.

My mother explained, "Ingrid, we have some ideas about getting your paper dolls replaced, not *all* of them, but many of them. We feel badly that they were accidentally thrown out and we appreciate how much they brightened your day. So, we put our allowance together and decided we could get you several new sets and the rest, all of us, can make ourselves. Some of us can draw the dolls on cardboard, others can draw some clothes. In fact, I'll make the mother dolls and clothes."

"And," my father said, "I'll make the father dolls and soldier uniforms. "

"And we'll make all the kids and their outfits,"concluded my sisters. "We'll just collect some paper, scissors and coloring crayons and start right in," they all agreed.

I couldn't speak because I was so overjoyed and so absolutely happy. Through happy tears, I finally said as I hugged everybody, "You are all the most wonderful, wonderful family a girl could have, and you're invited to play with me and my paper dolls any time you want."

As we were hugging, the air raid sirens sounded again and together we closed the blackout curtains, hoping that our efforts would help to keep all of us safe from a world at war.

Meet Me in St. Louis

I left my favorite home, the one that was on the Barge Canal. I had no choice. I didn't want to leave, but what could I do? I was just a kid and kid's opinions do not count for much. I hear people say there's no sense in crying over spilled milk, but our new house wasn't as nice. Well, maybe it was, it was just different. It was the top level of a two story flat and the wallpaper in the front room was dark purple with white grasshoppers on it, or maybe they were white flowers, I'm not sure, but I hated it. I was glad we were able to fit the piano in that room though, and there were plenty of bedrooms, the usual living and dining room, but mainly, my mother's "dream come true room:" a walk-in pantry, with floor to ceiling glass doors. You could tell how happy she was if anyone even mentioned the kitchen; she would light up and sing praises about her walk-in pantry. While we were still settling in, I met a girl in the neighborhood who was my age, named Ann. She was a big girl, not really overweight, just big and kind of shy. In fact, in the beginning, I had to do most of the talking, which I didn't mind, becausc (as I've been told) I like to talk. We'd get together some days after school and once in a while on a weekend. We'd play with my paper dolls or coloring books, then occasionally, we'd go to her house.

Ann's family was different from mine. We were two parents and three sisters. Ann had a father, (whom I called by his last name, Mr. Johnstone) who was really big, not fat, just tall and large. She had a step-mother, named Jessie, who was short and rotund and an older brother, named Raymond, who hid girly magazines under his bed. During that time, girly magazines were pictures of girls in skimpy swimsuits. We know because we used to sneak into his room and giggle over the pictures, convinced that we were engaging in sinful behaviors. Raymond also brought home black, velvet sofa pillows collected during his years in the Navy.

Sometimes I would be invited for dinner and Ann's stepmother would load up the plates in the kitchen and carry each one to the dining room table. She probably had to carry one at a time, because they were so loaded with food. I realized they were big people and therefore probably ate a lot, but each plate would be overflowing with mounds of mashed potatoes with a recessed pool of chicken ala king floating in the middle and spilling over the sides. It didn't take long to devour, for they used large tablespoons and didn't talk while they were scooping it in. Second helpings were always waiting in the wings.

Ann's mother would ask me, "C'mon, what's the matter with you? You eat like a bird. You're going to waste away to nothing."

I was always happy when dinner was over, and I was on my way home and then straight to my room to lie down upon my bed until all that food found a resting place in my gut and hopefully settled down. Lying there, I would swear, each time, to never say "yes" again to one of their dinner invitations, but aside from gargantuan portions, it *was* delicious.

High on the list of fun stuff to do was saving our weekly allowance to buy a round trip bus trip to the movies. During the era of World War II, the price of one movie ticket included:

two full-length movies, RKO Pathe News, several cartoons, previews and an adventure short (that was always continued the next week) such as "The Perils of Pauline." The shorts were called "cliff hangers" because that is literally where you left the hero or heroine – hanging from the edge of a cliff. Somehow, they always escaped. The lead role of a major film was usually a popular and well-known actor, one whose picture we cut out of movie magazines that we (with parent permission), hung on our bedroom walls. Charlie Chan, Peter Lorie, Sydney Greenstreet and Humphrey Bogart were usually the menacing "tough guys" in the mystery movies, along with the singing stars of the films: Judy Garland, Dina Shore, Frank Sinatra, Bing Crosby, Deanna Durbin, Katherine Grayson and forever on and on in one glorious, uplifting musical after another. Serious composers were writing the lasting and haunting music of then, today and tomorrow, from Cole Porter's "Night and Day" to Irving Berlin's "White Christmas." Of course, Ann and I knew all the stars, the songs and dialogue or script, from each movie. On the bus-ride home from our movie adventure, we would begin work on the musical we just saw and would plan to present to a captive audience – our family. We each chose the roles we wanted to play (sometimes playing 3-4 roles each, even more). Upon our arrival home, we began our performance, inviting family members to a first time, unrehearsed "run through." Like so many other young girls, it was helpful that we were both taking acrobat and tap dancing classes, preparing us, (we must have thought) for our lives as rich and famous movie stars.

Those were some of the fun times with Ann, but I have not mentioned some strange feelings I had, regarding the way she and her family behaved towards one another; sometimes harsh, and angry. There were times when I left her home that I sensed a feeling of relief.

There were several occasions when I noticed Ann would have a bruise on an arm or leg, or scratches on her face. I also recall there were times when she combed her hair, it seemed as though she had a good deal of hair in her comb. When I questioned her, she would lightly brush off the bruises and scratches, saying: "Oh, that's nothing," or "I fell," or "The cat scratched me." On a few occasions, Ann would lose her temper and push or shove me, but then quickly regained her composure and apologized.

In spite of my occasional uneasiness, I did not say "no" when Ann asked me if I would like to spend a weekend with her and her family on Sodus Bay, on Lake Ontario. Of course, I had to ask my parents, who, after talking with Ann's parents, agreed to the weekend.

Shortly after our arrival at a small cottage on the water, Ann's stepmother and a family friend, a Mr. Kramer, were sharing a bottle of whiskey. It could be that they had also been drinking during the drive to the lake, for now they were talking loudly, shouting, arguing and not able to walk without stumbling. Ann's father didn't appear to be drinking and made some attempts to quiet his wife and friend, while getting the grill ready for our hot dogs. Ann's stepmother, became more and more belligerent, so by the time we sat down by the lake to eat our dinner, I had quite lost my appetite which was replaced by a knot in my stomach and twinges of fright in my chest. When Mr. Johnstone asked Ann and me if we wished to start getting ready for bed, I think he could see we were and showed us to our room. I think I must have looked as though I was near tears because once we were in the bedroom, he took a moment to explain that Jessie would quiet down now and everything would be OK. He suggested we might want to take a book to bed, which was a double bed and I would be lying on the "inside" or next to the wall. After he left the room, we could hear him talking, not loudly, but sternly and things did quiet down. We read for a little while, talked quietly and then eventually drifted off.

It seemed to suddenly start up again: the screaming, shouting, banging of fists, furniture falling over and then our bedroom door flung open with Jessie lumbering through, a huge dark shadow in the doorway, bent over and making a lunge for Ann, shouting, "Where is that no good for nothing brat?" Her arms flailing and punches hitting Ann everywhere, slapping and twisting and pulling…..

I forced myself up against the bedroom wall, as far away as I could get, hanging onto the mattress, crying out, "Stop It! Stop It! Leave Her Alone!" and fearing that any minute one of those awful punches would be landing on me. Mr. Johnstone finally barged in and dragged Jessie out of the room, pulling her to a bedroom on the other side of the cottage, or so I guessed as her voice gradually died down.

Ann was sobbing, and I held her for awhile, but I wasn't sure how badly she was hurt and then her father came in and checked her over and made a determination that she didn't need a doctor or a hospital. I was so shaken I could hardly talk and asked Mr. Johnstone: "Are….are…you sure.....all…is ok? what if she comes back and starts to….starts to…. what if, are we safe now?" He assured me we were, went to get some lemonade for us and stayed in the room, in a lounge chair, and promised he would stay there until we were asleep or for the night, if necessary.

I awoke early, and while getting dressed and packing, told Ann I was going to call my parents and have them come and get me. She was sorry to see me go, but didn't blame me the least little bit.

I spoke to my parents and asked them to come and get me and take me home. I didn't tell them the whole story over the phone, but from what I did explain, I guess they could tell it was pretty important.

They must have really hurried, because it seemed like a very short time went by and they arrived. My father had a few words with Ann's father, who apologized many times and we all said goodbye, then left rather quickly. Before I left I told Ann how sorry I was for her and hoped things would get better within her family.

I probably saw Ann a few times after that night at the cottage on the lake, for our relationship had just become too uncomfortable. I later recalled how she had pushed me or shoved me when we had a disagreement, reflecting, I could see now, the behavior of some of her family. I guess that, sometimes, we don't do as our parents *tell* us, we do as they *do*.

I'll always view my relationship with Ann as bittersweet. We were able to use our talents and enjoy each other but there will always be a feeling of loss, especially with the troubled and uncertain ending; the ending of our friendship, seeking closure, but finding none. I wonder if she was able to let go of the abuse she suffered and had the opportunity to find a role in a more tender story, similar to the parts of the musicals and shows of our younger years; a story with a sweeter melody and kinder lyrics.

It is common when reminiscing about a relationship, to return to one or several occasions or remembrances and my favorite would be: "Ann, you did a great rendition of Judy Garland singing "The Trolley Song" from "Meet Me in St. Louis,("Louie, meet me at the fair….)"

The Dollhouse

Her name was Janet and she was incredible; she was cheerful, bubbly, happy and always a joy to be with. Being with her and visiting with her was like stepping through the window of a richly decorated hand carved Russian Easter egg, where inside was a new and different world of secret enchantment. Her parents were Danish like mine, so there were many ways we all had in common and many reasons to get along very well (which, by the way, we did). The best invitation I could ever receive was to spend a weekend at her house. She didn't live miles and miles away, but far enough so that my parents would drive me to her home Friday night and pick me up on Sunday afternoon. For me, upon arrival, it was like entering a magic castle, not really, I'm kind of exaggerating, but not far from the truth.

Janet was an only child and with all her worldly possessions, she should have been awfully spoiled – but, she wasn't. As far as I could see, she had all the toys and playthings, games and books and equipment for fun, that any young girl her age could possibly desire and indeed, it seems it all found a way to her home. There was never a problem with her sharing her collections, as she freely did so, without being asked. Many times she told me, "While you are here this weekend, everything I own is yours too."

Janet was not the only person who shared. Every time her mom would walk into our room, she was carrying a tray of little sandwiches, cookies, fruits and heavenly beverages with multi-colored straws in glasses decorated with brightly colored daisies and roses. I didn't even have to *think* about being hungry or thirsty and my wants were met. All meals at her home seemed special to me. It would be normal after a full day of non-stop play, to be called to the dining table for a full course turkey dinner with all the accompaniments, including a buffet of desserts – and it wasn't even Thanksgiving.

The weekend would start with entering her elegantly decorated bedroom with its white flouncy bedspread with ruffles that continued up the four posts ending in the matching canopy, softly draping above the entire bed. Wide bright pink ribbons and bows traveled along the seams of the spread and the overhead canopy.

Matching curtains also had pink bows, and placed in several areas of the room were large chests to hold her toys. The bed was so inviting. I was thrilled with the very idea of sleeping in that plush, deep, flouncy bed which we soon put to the test of accepting our bounces and jumps, very lightly done, of course. And her closet! I just loved looking into her closet, which to me, looked like a department store of exclusive designer dresses, with matching everything, including gloves, shoes, hats, and scarves. It was the largest wardrobe I had ever seen, but I was never really jealous of Janet and all her treasures. Maybe that was because she so willing to gave me full opportunities to play with whatever I pleased.

Finally, we were ready to "let the games begin!" In one weekend we had endless choices of how to enjoy ourselves: we would warm up by playing a few board games, followed by playing "zoo" with all of her stuffed animals, playing "mothers" by dressing and undressing selected dolls and taking them for walks in their separate English prams, to the basement for ping pong, and bowling games, playing grown ups with clothes from the trunk of ornate costumes, including high heeled shoes and huge feathery hats, and/or performing a ballet or even a one act play, for her parents (who sat in the audience with all the stuffed animals and dolls. The toys were certainly attentive, but not too great on the applause side).

My many visits were sure to include some days during the Christmas season. Her stately tree was covered with lamps of painted figures from the Disney collection including Mickey Mouse, Pluto, Donald Duck, Bambi and SnowWhite. One quiet evening I was standing by the Bambi lamp, looking at Bambi's big brown eyes and spotted fur coat, when Janet came over and stood next to me, took my hand in hers and asked, "Would you like to take that lamp home with you when you leave?" I was so touched by her gesture that it brought tears to my eyes and I smiled and said, "I would love to take it with me and put it on my tree and that would be a reminder of our friendship." It was a wonderful gesture, but not surprising for Janet. She seemed happiest when she was making other people happy.

Then, to the out of doors to continue our many activities, weather permitting, for roller skating or cross country skiing or ice skating and that's just a good beginning. Everything I mentioned was glorious fun, but it was not the best. The greatest, the most wonderful thing to do, ever, was to - - - *play with her doll house!*

I had never seen a doll house in my entire life. The first time

I saw it, we were finishing lunch and Janet's mom said, "Janet, aren't you going to show Ingrid your doll house?"

"A doll house?" I said. "What in the world is a doll house"

"Oh, Ingrid, I think you'll like it," said Janet's mom. "Janet's father made it especially for her. A dollhouse is a house just for very little people and inside of their house, they have almost everything we have in our house, only smaller. I'll call Janet's father and have him bring it down from the attic and put into Janet's room. We don't usually keep it there, because it takes up too much room."

"Why don't you girls take some cookies with you and enjoy them while you play with the house?"

We entered Janet's room and I could not believe my eyes! Before me was a huge two story home, with outside porches and decks and pools, and a barbeque area and picnic places and inside staircases to the basement and upstairs, and electric lights and …and…."Janet," I squealed, "it even has a doorbell that rings, I mean chimes!"

There were three or four bedrooms, playroom, den, living and dining room, fully stocked kitchen, laundry room and…… "Ingrid, my mother decorated the entire inside, with my help, of course and at Christmas time, we put up a tree by the fireplace," explained Janet.

"Now," Janet continued, "here are all the little plastic people. You just go ahead and pick out whichever ones you want to be and then you can talk for them."

We played with the doll house right up until dinner time, and right after dinner and until her mom and dad said we should get ready for bed and select our books for reading time. I swear, I could have played all night and when we had our nighties on and were saying goodnight, I said, " I really, truly, thank you for giving me such a good time today with Janet, and especially the doll house."As I said my prayers that night, I gave thanks for having such a good friend as Janet.

We read our books for awhile, talking and giggling in between pages, until, finally, our eyes started to close. We agreed that the good fairy of sleepyland was inviting us to follow her.

I woke up earlier than I usually do, mainly, I think, because the bed felt different. I put my hands out above the covers and felt around for the pink bows, and felt none.That made me feel kind of funny, so I carefully peeked through my sleepy eyelids, looking for the canopy and saw none! What is going on here? Where did the plush, lush, bedclothes go? I sat up in bed, looked around the room and realized that though it looked it familiar, it was in a strange kind of way. Janet's chest of toys was not there and the open closet doors revealed none of the beautiful dresses or accessories. How could it look familiar, as though I had seen it before? I hated to wake Janet, but I felt that if I didn't talk about this, soon, I might start to get scared, I mean, very scared.

"Janet," I whispered, at first, "Janet, are you awake?

"Mfm-m-m-m-," she replied.

"Janet, you've got to wake up, something goofy or very strange has happened."

"OK, OK, Ingrid, I'm awake, but barely. What happened? What's the matter?'

"I'm not sure," I replied. "But unless I'm wrong, I think we're in a different bed and different room than the one in which we went to sleep."

Janet did not respond and was very quiet, for a long time. Finally, she said, "You know, I think you're right. If I'm not mistaken, and don't necessarily believe me, because this is too weird, but this looks like the master bedroom in my doll house!"

"Janet. I don't know what to say, but I think we really are in, I mean, actually inside your dollhouse! Don't ask me why and don't ask me how, but that's what I think!

"Ingrid," Janet replied, "I've heard about magic and strange experiences and how do we know? Maybe this is one of those happenings. Could be you're right! Why don't we quietly and carefully, crawl out of bed and look around the house?"

We agreed to investigate and tiptoed, at first, through the house, looking in most of the rooms and found that everything looked normal – normal for a dollhouse.

Becoming more and more upset, Ingrid, near tears, said, "So everything looks like a normal doll house except for us. We've shrunk! We're so tiny, we fit perfectly into this house! Plus, when we went to sleep last night, it was in *your own bedroom,* in *your house and not here, in the doll house!* I, for one, would like to leave this house, like, right now! I'll meet you at the front door, because that is exactly where I'm going and I'm going to run right through the door and out of here – *now!"*

Both girls ran to the front door, grasped the door knob only to discover it would not turn. No matter how they tried, the door refused to open. They went to nearby windows and discovered they were not able to unlock any of them.

"Ingrid, I'm really scared because I think this house is trying to keep us here against our will. I don't know what's happened, but could it be that this house has become an evil house? You know, like a haunted house, but this time, a doll house that tries to scare children! I can't explain it but we need to get out of here! Let's run to the bedroom where we slept last night, I think there's a phone there and if it still works, let's call my parents." Once they arrived in the bedroom, Janet, now trembling, picked up the phone and dialed her number, realizing at the same time, they were in her own bedroom and not in the doll house. When her mother finally answered, Janet started shouting into the phone: "*Mother, dad, come and get us, help us……..the doll house, I mean, I think it's the doll house, but it looks like our house, won't let us out!! Oh, I'm all mixed up, I don't know what I'm saying!!!…."*

And within a few minutes, the door opened and Janet's mom and dad rushed in, asking: "Girls, what is the matter? What has happened?" Were you having a nightmare?"

We threw our arms around them and hugged until we thought we'd never let go. At this point, though we were quite upset, we were trying to figure out what had happened. We looked around the bedroom and saw it was, indeed, Janet's room, with the white canopy and pink bows. We realized we were both reading the same story before going to sleep. "Do you suppose it's possible for two people to have similar dreams?" I asked Janet.

Janet said, "I never heard of such a thing happening, but I guess it could, and I wonder if we could have been sleep walking when we explored the doll house, or was that just part of the dream?"

"But, it was terrible," we explained. "We were trapped in the house and couldn't get out! From now on, it we ever have that dream again, let's be sure to unlock all the doors so we can get out." That sounded so silly, and maybe in the future we would be able to laugh about it, but not right now. We started to calm down, but found ourselves repeatedly looking around the bedroom, as if to convince ourselves that what we saw was Janet's room, with the white canopy with pink bows. We later talked about that dream many times, finding it a bit difficult to completely forget.

Janet would sometimes stay over at my house and we would be included on all day bicycle trips with the adults, and there were picnics and swimming at the beaches.

It wasn't very long after our last picnic, that Janet told me that her family, her parents and she, were moving out of the state. Her father had had a job promotion, and they felt it was a good opportunity for them. So then, the next time I visited Janet at her house, we both understood it would be the last time, that is, until our parents made the drive to one another's house. For the last time, on our final weekend, we played with the dollhouse again, remembering our weird and funny dream as well as all the fun times we had with it.

We played in our usual fun fashion with just a hint of sadness. We agreed, of course, to phone and write, but it was still a tearful goodbye. I left to go to the car and was about to get in, when I saw a large object in the back seat:

It was the doll house! Right there, taking up most of the back seat!

"Janet!" I cried out..."I can't take your dollhouse! What will you do without it?"

"Ingrid, that doll house is yours. My dad said he would make me another, I if want, and besides, I want you to have this one. It would make me very happy."

"Oh, Janet, thank you, thank you, thank you. And every time I play with it, I'll think of all the wonderful times we had together and maybe that way, I won't miss you so much. I just love you, Janet. '"

"I love you, too, Ingrid,"

Ingrid looked out the front window and returned Janet's wave, both happily, yet sadly, smiling at one another. Ingrid thought of the beautiful doll house and how much fun they had with it and here it was, right next to her in the back seat.

"I can't wait," she thought, "to put the doll house into my bedroom."

But somehow, deep within Ingrid, a queasy, uneasy feeling started stirring, something like a combination of fear, horror, fascination and an overpowering urge to fun as fast as she could, from the doll house and never look back.....

"Oh, I'm just being silly," she thought – "it was only a dream.....wasn't it?"

All About Buses

The Bus And The Frog

In the beginning of my life when I rode buses, I thought they were terrible old things, chugging and hissing and rattling and creaking. I would hold my mother's hand as we waited at the bus stop and when I saw the approaching bus, I was sure it was headed straight for me. I tightened my grip and squeezed her hand as hard as I could and she would say, "It's OK, Ingrid. Don't be frightened – I'll help you board the bus." The bus would make a loud, squealing braking sound, doors would part in the middle and open to the sides and I would carefully step up the stairs. Not all drivers were nice. Some even looked a little grumpy, but this driver was special because he would sing fun songs whenever a little kid, like me, would get on the bus.

"Ingrid," he would say, "what song would you like to hear today?"

After we settled in the double side seat, near the driver, I thought for a minute and said, "Oh, I'd love to hear the frog song. Would you please sing that one for me?"

Looking out the huge front window of the bus, we could see the snow had started to drift down in dreamy circles and the driver said, "Looks like we need a frog to bring a bit of spring to us!" and bellowed right into the first line:

"A frog went a-courtin,' he did ride. Ring- tum- bodi- mit-cha- cam-bow. A sword and a butler by his side. Ring- tum-bodi- mit- cha- cam- bow. A straddle- adle- adle- bobel a-dle-bobel link- tum, Ring- tum- bodi- mit- cha- cam-bow."

Of course, we didn't have any idea what all the words meant, but we didn't care, because they were so much fun to sing.

He seemed to enjoy the singing as much as we did and would add verse after verse and after awhile, upon his urging, most of the passengers were singing along with us. When he finished, we would all clap and shout, "More, more!" What a fun bus ride! How was it possible that old gray bus turned into Cinderella's coach and four?

The Bus To Toyland

Mostly, I adored our bus trip, with my mother and two sisters, to the shopping district during the Christmas season. There was so much to do and say and sing and smile (seems as though everyone smiled at Christmas time). There were busy people shopping and crowds and money passing back and forth, but my particular thrill was the special Christmas display on the second floor of the Sibley Department store. As we approached the exhibit, the lights started to dim and the hallway narrowed down to a dark tunnel that soon opened up to a wide walkway lit up with *millions* of tiny colored lights, shining on fifteen or more huge glass window displays with life-size figures inside depicting scenes of the season. As we shuffled slowly along, we waved to Santa Claus in one window and baby Jesus and the three wise men in another. The last three windows displayed all sorts of toys to the tune of "Toyland." We never saw so many toys that were dancing, rolling, talking, sliding; toys and trains and boats and blocks for building or paints for coloring books and games to play on boards, (trillions of board games) and my favorite toy – books and books of paper dolls, all just waiting to be carefully cut out and assembled. and…and…oh, my - I guess I did slow down my pace, as our mother reminds us, stating: "All right, girls, let's not hold up the line; we must move along now."

The Bus That Went To Music School

Buses and their drivers became my friends. At times, if the driver didn't see me, or others, waiting at our usual stop, by our usual time, he would slow down and he and the passengers would scan the side streets and sometimes you'd hear someone shout, "There she is! Here she comes! Hey, Ingrid – Hurry up!"

Every Saturday morning I boarded the 10:00 a.m. bus that would deliver me to the door of the Eastman School of Music. I always had homework, (in music theory and composition), which I always wanted to check out one more time before class. The problem was, when a bus started to get too old, which made the ride too bumpy, it was sometimes near impossible to write eighth notes and sharps and flats, or any revision, during the 45 minute bus trip. But then, sometimes, I was relieved if the bus was old and slow, for it gave me more time to really finish the music.

A Date On A Bus

When I was around 12-13 years old, I went on my first date and of course, on a bus. Today, I would most likely describe the event as the most *socially uncomfortable* bus ride I ever had, but frankly, I don't think I would have known the meaning of those words. I only knew that a *first date,* at that age was unheard of and I can see why. My date, Bob Miller was one of my classmates. We were both in the 7th grade and out of nowhere, he telephoned me and asked if I would like go to a movie with him. We knew absolutely nothing about dating and even though our parents approved, it was just awful. I don't know why I said "yes," and almost immediately, I was sorry that I accepted. We stood five feet apart at the bus stop, staring off into opposite directions and not speaking one word. To make matters worse, on the way home, a group of our classmates boarded the same bus. We suffered no obvious teasing as they probably never assumed we were even together (except maybe, I did hear some faint giggling). As I look back and try to understand the whole experience, all I can say is it was probably just one of those countless little mistakes adolescents make when they are trying not to be adolescents.

A Bus For Christmas Eve

I was waiting, by myself, on Christmas Eve, for a bus to take me to our church service. In the distance, I could hear carolers sweetly singing the familiar holiday songs. I was standing at a bus stop under a street lamp whose light reflected from the frozen ground crusted white with icy snow. Wherever it shone, sparkles were born, glimmered around me and upon me and I couldn't help but think this truly was a special night for I had never seen such dancing white lights. Gradually, the heavens above me let go of the most enviable creation of snow flakes, one after another until soon, the world was adorned with white petals of snow coming to rest on the shoulders of carolers and under street lamps everywhere. Adding to the majesty of the scene, I felt positively uplifted in my new red hat, white, silk scarf and new black coat.

While I was waiting for the bus and anticipating the church service, with its the candlelight, flowers, and the choirs singing the Christmas music, I sensed I was becoming more and more integrated with the ceremony, a deeper part, perhaps, of the spiritual drama of Christmas Eve. There was also another part of me that had to admit that I was wondering, just a little, about the cute tenor in the second row of the boys' choir.

My Old Friend, The Bus

Even though I was a little nervous, the lady said I did well and gave me a small piece of blue paper and told me to give it to my parents, which I did. The lady was a hygienist who cleaned our teeth. Several times a year, a team of ladies would visit our school and not only clean our teeth, but report any teeth that needed attention. In several weeks or so, I discovered that the piece of blue paper meant I would join a group of children, board a bus at our school and accompanied by a teacher, were bussed to the Public Dental Dispensary. All of us were going to see a dental student.

The dispensary was the biggest, tallest, darkest, scariest place I had ever seen and when I got off the bus, I thought I heard it growl at me, in a low guttural warning sound. I was instructed to enter the front doors and stepped inside a huge room that smelled of iodine, with white walls and white tile floors with huge chandeliers hanging down from miles above me and attached to starburst designs on the ceiling. I was told to sit down on a wooden bench, to be quiet and listen for my name to be called. I had no idea what was going to happen or what was going to be done to us. I did as I was told. We were sitting by a staircase and shortly a man, dressed in white at the top of the staircase called out my name. I was so startled I jumped to my feet and quickly started to climb the stairs, holding onto a railing I could hardly get my hand around. The man grabbed my arm and roughly shoved me down a long hall that was full of rows of white and brown monster chairs.

"Climb up here," he ordered. This was the first time I could see him clearly. He looked strange. He had bristly short dark hair, with a puffy round face and small narrow eyes, glowering at me. He bent over me and looked into my mouth and poked at me in many wrong places and I said, "Ouch!" He grabbed a white towel and slapped me across my face, hard, giving the towel a loud snap and shouted, " Shut up!"

I was scared and mad. My face was stinging and I was crying: one tear chasing another down cheeks. I am not sure what happened after that, except he told me to go back down the stairs and report to my teacher, which I did, as fast as I could.

After that experience, I never went to the Dispensary again. For whenever I received a blue slip and was told to give it to my parents, I went to a door marked "Girls" tore up the slip of blue paper and flushed it down the toilet. When my parents asked about my teeth cleaning, I said everything went just fine. Of course, my little game was eventually discovered.

When all of us had been seen for our appointment, we were assembled outside to wait for the bus to drive us back to school. As we boarded the bus, you never saw so many tears turn to smiles so fast, because, there was my favorite bus driver, who, when he saw my tears, said, "C'mon, Ingrid, sit up here by me and we'll sing the frog song together, shall we? You know, the one that went: a frog went a-courtin'-he did ride……. ring-tum- bodi- mit- che- cam - -bow. A sword and a butler by his side…….."

"Oh, thank you. Wow, am I ever glad to see you!" I said. "You are truly the best bus driver of them all!" And pretty soon, not a one of us was crying and all of us were singing "a frog… .."went a-courtin'... he did ride......ring- tum- bodi- mitcha-cambow……."

Prelude

I had such mixed feelings as I sat in the section of the auditorium reserved for the graduating class and their parents, of the Preparatory School of the Eastman School of Music. Since we had arrived a little early, I indulged in a few moments of reminiscing, how I came to be in this exact place, this time, this moment, this year. While I attended elementary and high school, I was also enrolled in the Preparatory School of the Eastman School of Music studying piano, theory, music history and numerous related subjects. Every year of my enrollment, I had met the requirements for honor student status, which required, in addition to other criteria, a specified number of minutes in performance in the classroom and in Kilborne Hall-an elegant recital hall of the school. The harder I studied, the more my love of music and the piano grew, always nourishing my dream to achieve the status of a concert pianist. My instructors had always encouraged me to pursue a career at the piano for they believed I had the talent to achieve success.

I took a moment, again, to scan the program for today's graduation and lingered over my name listed under "Honor Students" and again wondered how I possibly could have received such a response to my application to the college level of the Eastman School of Music, the very school for which I had successfully prepared!

I had applied to the college a few months ago, had now just graduated from high school and finally, after months of waiting, received a letter from the Admissions Department that stated: "We regret to inform you that….." "W H A T ?"

"We regret to inform you that we are unable to accept your application"...."WHAT?!"

"WRONG, WRONG PERSON, WRONG RECORD, mix-up of records, impossible,... HOW?

Emerging from states of disbelief and shock, I was left with a dismal apprehension that my dreams of performing as a concert pianist might have just suffered a serious blow. I promptly contacted the school requesting an explanation for denying admission to one of their own students,(albeit a different department) currently graduating with honors from the Preparatory Department.

Several weeks have transpired since my inquiry and now, as of this date, this time, in this very chair and sitting next to my parents, who, are also mystified with my graduation and ensuing letter of refusal, my inquiry remains unanswered. A condition which will not change if I take just a moment to introduce you to my parents, for without their story, the remainder of these events will not be clearly understood, nor will the impact it had upon the rest of my life be understood.

My parents were immigrants from Denmark, born in Copenhagen. My father stood 6' tall, proud and with handsome features. He was schooled in English, consequently he spoke with a studied style with a rather attractive Danish accent. He always had an air of confidence about him, with exquisite manners typical of a gentleman, towards men or towards women. When I was little, I remember he taught me to properly greet someone to whom I was introduced, he would say, "First, you always look the person in the eyes, smile a little, extend your hand to shake theirs, say, "How do you do, while bending over ever so slightly from the waist." He would further explain, "When you look a person in the eye, it shows you respect him." I was witness to this gentleman's behavior and saw, personally, how my father was honored and respected by those who worked with him. He was employed by the University of Rochester Medical School, interacted with the medical staff and physicians throughout his 50+ years of employment and was always held in the highest level of regard. My apology for getting side-tracked with an added note. My father didn't just *pretend* to respect others, he genuinely did and it showed.

We are still sitting here, in the section reserved for the graduating students and their parents, awaiting the arrival of the guest speaker. I quickly glance at my mother who is sitting next to me, waiting patiently for the ceremonies to begin. She raised me in both Danish and English languages, and I started to recall her significance in my world of music.

She was a very pretty lady with dark brown wavy hair and heavenly blue eyes. She was 5' or a little less, of small structure, but so quick and light that she at one time won a city championship in the badminton tournaments. I think that says a good deal about her. To further acknowledge that feat, she was a person of determination and conviction of her sense of right and wrong. This was not easy for her due to her difficulty with the English language, which would make it much more challenging to stand up for your principles when hampered with unfamiliar word choices. An appropriate example: there was a brief period during my studies at the piano, when I was afflicted with a minor illness and experienced a common lack of self-will, following my recovery, to get back into the practicing mode. For no matter how deeply the love of the art, practicing is always hard work, requiring discipline and determination. Since an adolescent always knows best, I informed my parents I would not be returning to the music school and needed more time for socializing. Our discussions failed to change my mind. Arriving at the school immediately prior to my final piano lesson, I received a note from the office of the Director of the Preparatory Department, a Dr. Raymond Wilson, instructing me to promptly report to his office. I did. I was ushered into a huge office, walled in dark brown draperies, very low, soft lighting, with a gigantic walnut desk far at one end and there, sitting behind the desk, the very head, himself, of the Preparatory Department. And over to one side of the desk, in a leather upright chair, sat *my mother!* The director informed me that my mother felt so strongly about my ability and was so convinced of my potential, that she could not accept my decision to terminate my studies, especially since I had been spending so little time practicing. (Which was true, due to my illness, said I). The director asked how much time I usually spent practicing and I told him. My mother said half of that time and following a long, long story with mild disagreements, the director expressed his amazement that I had progressed so far with such little practice. By the end of our discussion, I agreed not only to return to my studies, but to significantly increase my hours of practice. I silently swore to myself to never, ever, speak to my mother again, in English or Danish or in any language for as long as I lived! Later, that night, I was able to place myself in her position; socially insecure because of the language problem, not able to drive, requiring that she take herself "to town by bus," to the imposing and impressive school of music, discussing her concerns with the director and preparing herself for her daughter's hostility and certainly, lack of appreciation. I did thank her and apologized for not understanding her motives and love. The entire experience, I later came to realize, was just another example of how her courage helped to shape the rest of my life.

The time was nearing for the commencement to begin, yet the guest speaker was still not in attendance, so my memory banks continued to unravel.

My parents were artistically talented. Both of them had the creative gene; our family history was populated with artists of canvases, of music and my sister closest to me in age was an exceptional artist in whatever medium she chose, (oils, water colors, ink, charcoal) in addition to sculpting magnificent figures of stone. My oldest sister continues her love of the art of T'aiChi and yoga, still conducting classes in the park on cool mornings near Stockholm, Sweden at the age of 82.

Musical evenings of either solo performance, or duets and quartets were common in our household. It was usual to have my father seated at the piano, playing and singing harmony to my mother's sweet soprano voice, with any one of our Danish friends at the violin, mandolin or zither. There were Danish songs to sing, World War II songs to sing, folk songs to sing and folk dances to dance. And if the music wasn't live, there was always the phonograph playing Lawrence Melchoir or Victor Borge or Rachmoninoff, or, ...I loved it! It was heaven to me! It was pure joy!

In particular, my mother had an uncanny sense for the classics. Often, when I practiced Bach, Beethoven, or Mozart at home (vs the practice rooms in the school) she would sit on the side lines, listening, enjoying and then would step over to the keyboard and point out where she heard that "something" wasn't right, wrong note, or wrong rhythm. I politely tolerated her advice until my instructor would later point out the exact area of which my mother spoke which never failed to amaze me. Moreover, she was not just listening to criticize, but for hours, she would listen to me play music from the masters, from popular tunes of the day, sight reading volumes of music books, sharing our own music wonderland. Such concerts were always a delightful experience, and I was truly unaware how fortunate I was to be surrounded with such music.

My reminiscing has been focusing in and out of reality, for in-between recollections, a speaker has opened the program and another gentleman is calling out the names of the graduates who have been proceeding to the stage to receive their diplomas. Finally, my name is called. I look the keeper of the diplomas in the eye, smile, bend ever so slightly and say, "Thank you," and resume my place next to my parents.

.... "and today's speaker, will be the Director of The Eastman School of Music, Dr. Howard Hanson." He could hardly be called a "guest" speaker, for he was none other, besides a famous composer, famous musician and leader of the music world, our very own President, Director of the whole music school. He was the top. He was the one in charge and through him, all must flow, music or otherwise. He finished his commencement address, I listened, proud of my achievement and sat there, chin to chest, not smiling, fingering my diploma (with honors) and, I couldn't help it, I tried, but I couldn't stop the tears from trickling down my cheeks. My mother looked at me. Dr. Hanson was accepting the applause for his address, bowed and started leaving the stage, making his way to the exit in the rear of the room, necessitating his passing by us, commencing down the very aisle leading to where we were sitting. I saw my mother touch my father's arm and I heard her say, "Ask him, when he comes by, stop him for just a minute," and I thought, in a state of extreme panic, "Oh my God, she's not telling dad to stop *HIM!*" I saw my father signal "no" and just as *HE* was about to pass by, my mother spoke out, "Oh, excuse me sir.." and my father quickly surmising what was about to happen, took over and softly introduced himself (looking into *HIS* eyes, I bet) and quietly, respectfully described the rejection by the very college, which today, was honoring my honor status. *HE* seemed genuinely interested, smiled at the three of us, offered *HIS* hand to me in congratulations for today's recognition of my achievement and said to my parents, "Someone will get in touch with you."

"Holy Cow! Jiminy Crickets! and God Bless America!" He actually stopped and spoke to us! He shook my hand! He said someone would be in touch with us! At first, when I guessed what my mother had in mind, I wanted to run out the back door, so afraid was I of offending the Director. But here was my mother, modest, shy and hardly well-spoken, marching up to Goliath, ready to explain that she could not accept a situation that she believed was not justified, was not right and regardless of the power and or might of the opposing force, was determined to speak out, to rectify a perceived wrong. Holy Cow! What a lady! The chances, on the surface, did not appear to be in our favor, yet, in spite of a probable negative outcome, both of my parents decided to take a risk in our behalf. I saw my mother, following her encounter with *HIMSELF,* through a somewhat different perspective. Though I always had seen her mainly as shy and timid, she certainly no longer appeared as such and I saw *HERSELF* with a new respect and admiration.

True to his word, in about one week I received a letter from Dr. Hansen, inviting me to appear at the studio of the Chairman of the Piano Department where I was welcome to perform a special audition recital, to be evaluated by the Chair (who was Cecil Genhardt,) who would submit her findings to Dr. Hansen. I was delighted to have the opportunity to prove myself. I was not delighted that I should be required to do so in the absence of any explanation. What had I done? What had I not done? Nonetheless I immediately assembled a program and embarked upon an intensive period of practice.

The fateful day arrived and I was once again in that position of waiting for my turn to perform. In this case, however, it was not backstage, but in the hallway outside the door to the Chairman's studio. Of course, I was nervous, but I had been in this time, place and circumstances many times before, so I knew exactly what I must do:

I began my special thinking of positive self-talk, such as: (thinking to myself: *"I am the best pianist in the entire world, no one can play better than I")* The door opened and I entered a room barely large enough for two persons and a Steinway grand. *("No one can play more beautifully than I")* A lady smiled and motioned towards the piano. *("I am the best, the absolute best")* I sat down on the bench, put my hands on the keys and the magic took over once again. My entire mind was the music, completely absorbed with it, taken over by it and I became at once, the performer and the listener. I was the creator of the music. I was the music. I was enthralled with the music. "Thank you. That will be all,"came a voice from the remote outskirts of the galaxy.

CLICK: mind reset to time: *now,* place: *here,* person: *me*. I arose from the piano bench, smiled, and accepted the opened door to the hallway as my cue to exit. I was elated. I had done well. It felt good and if that wasn't acceptable, then I was not acceptable. But I was, according to the letter from the director *(HIMSELF* again) which began, "I am pleased to inform you…………...and congratulate you upon your performance and your acceptance……..." *I did it!*…… Now, let the real work begin.

There was never a mention why I received a letter of regret and I decided, along with my parents, to let the matter rest and not pursue it any further.

I was honored to be included in a graduating class that included nine of us who completed a major in piano. No one said it was going to be easy, but when you're talking about dreams coming true…..is it ever….easy?

ABOUT THE AUTHOR

E. K. Williams, previously known as Ellen K. Williams, the author of her first book, entitled "Let's Go Around Again," now re- enters the literary scene as E. K. Williams with a new and second book entitled; "Sketches."

E. K. Williams continues to draw upon her Bachelor Degree in Music (piano) from Eastman School of Music and her Masters in Counseling, filtering her experiences and observations into her writings. She has performed, composed and taught music and during the last ten years of her professional history, practiced as a psychotherapist.

Her love of literature and earlier writings surfaced in recent years culminating into a desire to further explore her talents. She returns once more, with charming tidbits of wit, with figments of her vivid imagination, still provoking the reader's mind.

NOTABLE NOTES ABOUT THE AUTHOR

….."the writer is multi-talented, using her skills as a therapist and musician to weave tales of love, daily struggles and humor"…..Crossville Chronicle,……."her writings have a "tongue in cheek" quality, full of wit, humor, wisdom gleaned from years of clients,…." Wordgathering: ….her essay is about facing the reality of life one is living…insightful and perceptive……"Williams offers a collection of humorous and autobiographic essays, stories and poems…….from Rochester Review, University of Rochester. Williams has been a regular contributor to "Our Senior Times" has appeared in the Crossville Chronicle, The Glade Sun and Knoxville Sentinel.

THE END OF A BOOK

I just had an unexpected emotional reaction. That I had an emotional reaction is not unusual, but it was the event that prompted my response that so impressed me. I had started to scan the *Contents* of the chapters of my finished manuscript titled *Sketches*. I had finished it four days ago and at that time the entire one-hundred and sixty pages were sped off to the publishing company in Nashville. That is exactly what I was hoping and expecting to happen. With luck, I will soon receive an approval notice from the publishing house along with a first real live edition of my book, sent to me for my approval and acceptance.

I scanned the first section with its six chapters grouped together because the characters, no, because the *people* in those chapters were placed there due to their commonalities. As I scanned the chapter headings and began recalling who they were, what they had to say and why they were there, I found my rational thinking skills slipping over into the emotional side of my storytelling and perhaps due to my shock I was thinking of these people as my dear friends; people I had known, in some cases, for months and months. Some I molded and nurtured late at night in the quiet computer room, some even later, propped up in bed, searching for the right word, phrase, or expression to bring them to life. My relationship with them was not casual or superficial. In some cases I delved deeply into the inner workings of their mind or soul and the tears started brimming in my eyes. What sense does this make? I felt as though they were leaving me and we had been through so much together. We had worked *hard* together; rough drafting, stumbling in and out of feelings, revising, revising and revising again and sometimes, back to the beginning. It was not always my doing, or theirs, no one person or event was to blame. It was simply us, who we were that showed us the way. Many times we followed, not knowing where the stories, or the happenings would take us. In some chapters, even where my thoughts were the predominate theme, I was still not the conductor or the leader, for part of me was always involved within the setting, the scene, that showed me the direction or the way to travel.

I began to scan down the other chapters, remembering the laughter and the tears of the little kids, their fears and their joys. Even with chapters involving objects and not life forms were touching me– because they *are all alive to me* and now, I'm not so urgent or needed. They're finished and can stand alone. *Well, I still need them.* I'll read them over and each time recall how we felt when we found a short cut to serenity or talked with a rooster or listened to a Cherry tree weep.

What is in the book is and always will be a part of me and I thank each story, each rhyme or sketch that I assembled and orchestrated for being so patient and loving with me, in return.

CPSIA information can be obtained at www.ICGtesting.com
Printed in the USA
BVOW07s0734091213

338255BV00007B/17/P

9 780578 080093